# America's Magnificent Mountains

*Prepared by the* SPECIAL PUBLICATIONS DIVISION
NATIONAL GEOGRAPHIC SOCIETY, WASHINGTON, D. C.

## AMERICA'S MAGNIFICENT MOUNTAINS

*Contributing Authors:* LOUIS DE LA HABA,
   RALPH GRAY, SALLIE M. GREENWOOD,
   DANIEL E. HUTNER, GEORGE F. MOBLEY,
   H. ROBERT MORRISON, CHARLTON OGBURN,
   CYNTHIA RUSS RAMSAY
*Contributing Photographers:* JAMES P. BLAIR,
   NICHOLAS DEVORE III, DAVID FALCONER,
   FARRELL GREHAN, ANNIE GRIFFITHS,
   SARAH LEEN, GEORGE F. MOBLEY,
   GALEN ROWELL
*Published by*
   The National Geographic Society
   ROBERT E. DOYLE, *President*
   MELVIN M. PAYNE, *Chairman of the Board*
   GILBERT M. GROSVENOR, *Editor*
   MELVILLE BELL GROSVENOR, *Editor Emeritus*
*Prepared by*
   The Special Publications Division
   ROBERT L. BREEDEN, *Editor*
   DONALD J. CRUMP, *Associate Editor*
   PHILIP B. SILCOTT, *Senior Editor*
   MERRILL WINDSOR, *Managing Editor*
   MARY ANN HARRELL, *Consulting Editor*
   JOHN AGNONE, *Picture Editor*
   JODY BOLT, *Art Director*
   SALLIE M. GREENWOOD, MARILYN L. WILBUR,
      *Researchers;* KATHERYN M. SLOCUM, *Assistant
      Researcher*
*Illustrations and Design*
   SUEZ B. KEHL, *Assistant Art Director*
   CINDA ROSE, *Designer;* CYNTHIA BREEDEN,
      MARIANNE R. KOSZORUS, *Assistant Designers*
   ARTHUR J. COX, HARRY D. KAUHANE,
      MARY LATHAM, CHARLES MILLER,
      SALLY S. SUMMERALL, TIBOR G. TOTH,
      WALTER VASQUES, THOMAS A. WALSH,
      SUSAN YOUNG, *Cartography*
   JANE H. BUXTON, LOUIS DE LA HABA, RALPH GRAY
      SALLIE M. GREENWOOD, DANIEL E. HUTNER,
      H. ROBERT MORRISON, SUZANNE VENINO,
      *Picture Legends*
*Engraving, Printing, and Product Manufacture*
   ROBERT W. MESSER, *Manager*
   GEORGE V. WHITE, *Production Manager*
   JUNE L. GRAHAM, RICHARD A. MCCLURE,
      RAJA D. MURSHED, CHRISTINE A. ROBERTS,
      *Assistant Production Managers*
   DAVID V. SHOWERS, *Production Assistant*
   SUSAN M. OEHLER, *Production Staff Assistant*
   DEBRA A. ANTONINI, PAMELA A. BLACK,
      BARBARA BRICKS, JANE H. BUXTON,
      MARY ELIZABETH DAVIS, ROSAMUND GARNER,
      NANCY J. HARVEY, JANE M. HOLLOWAY, JOAN
      HURST, SUZANNE J. JACOBSON, ARTEMIS
      S. LAMPATHAKIS, CLEO PETROFF, MARCIA
      ROBINSON, KATHERYN M. SLOCUM,
      SUZANNE VENINO, *Staff Assistants*
   SARAH C. WERKHEISER, *Index*

GALEN ROWELL

*Stepping carefully in fresh powder snow,
Hank Bahnson descends Karstens Ridge
on North America's highest mountain—
20,320-foot Mount McKinley.*

PRECEDING PAGES: *Students from Aspen Middle
School practice snow-climbing techniques in
Colorado's Elk Mountains, a subrange of the
Rockies.* PAGE 1: *Jagged ridge leads toward
Gilbert Peak in Washington's Goat Rocks
Wilderness, a portion of the rugged Cascade
Range.* FRONT ENDPAPER: *Alpenglow colors
Mount McKinley at sunset as shadows
descend on lesser peaks of the Alaska Range.*
BACK ENDPAPER: *Morning clouds break
against ridges of 18,855-foot Pico de Orizaba
in central Mexico.*

PAGES 2-3: ANNIE GRIFFITHS; PAGE 1: FARRELL GREHAN;
FRONT ENDPAPER: PERRY RIDDLE; BACK ENDPAPER: GEORGE F. MOBLEY

# Foreword

T HE PATRIOTIC HYMN "America" is almost our second national anthem. With countless others I share the love it expresses for "thy woods and templed hills"; the highlands draw me back again and again. I have seen the first light of morning touch the top of Maine's Mount Katahdin, and watched the sun slip into the Pacific as I stood on Mount Tamalpais just north of the Golden Gate. Most spectacular of all was the midnight sun grazing the northern horizon, viewed from the hard-gained heights of Mount McKinley.

The wooded slopes of our eastern "templed hills" change with every season. Which is more dramatic, the exuberant late-spring bloom of the Smokies or the rich tapestry of autumn on the New England hills? Throughout the year the roads and trails of these venerable, peaceful ranges of the East attract the crowd-weary residents of nearby cities.

Our western mountains are of a different kind, younger and more massive, and as grand in beauty as in scale. My first venture into the Sierra Nevada in 1925 was along the John Muir Trail. I well remember the columbine and the Indian paintbrush in the meadows, and the rainbow and golden trout in the streams. For many, Yosemite National Park is the focal point of the Sierra. It is a fine choice, particularly in the springtime when the falls are full with snowmelt.

But I admit a predilection for the remote Coast Mountains of British Columbia. The splendid range leading up to Mount Waddington boasts deep forests, and glaciers that reach from the snowy peaks almost to sea level. This is a superb place for climbers to test their ardor and try their skills on both rock and ice. The region will never be crowded, for it is defended by distance, rain and snow, deep bush, and even an occasional grizzly bear.

I often wonder what place has given me the most lasting impression. Surely one candidate is Yosemite Valley. Another is the great bulk of Mount McKinley, rising more than three miles above the surrounding tundra. But fully as rewarding were much smaller, more intimate scenes known only to a few. What could equal the pleasure of watching an ouzel bobbing on a rock in the middle of a stream, or of examining the tiny, brilliant flowers of moss campion in the snow-ringed crevice of a rock? Above all else, such moments bring the realization of one's unity with nature.

The eight sections of this book capture the spirit of life and travel in the mountains. Its essential message is how people of all ages can be sustained by the highlands for a day, a few weeks, a lifetime. None is too young to start or too old to remember.

STERLING B. HENDRICKS
*Committee for Research and Exploration*
*National Geographic Society*

# Contents

*Glacier-fed Tuolumne
River flows through
Tuolumne Meadows in
Yosemite National Park,
California. Beyond, peaks
of the Sierra Nevada
beckon to backpackers,
rock-climbers, and
horsemen, many of
whom set off from here
to explore Yosemite's
high backcountry.*

7

# The Sierra Nevada

*Lowering veil of clouds screens the late spring sun over Kings Canyon National Park in*

*By* LOUIS DE LA HABA
*Photographed by* NICHOLAS DE VORE III

*California. Such tumbled, jagged scenery typifies much of the Sierra Nevada.*

*Thrusting aloft its tilted granite ridges and soaring peaks,* the Sierra Nevada extends more than 400 miles southeast from the Cascade Range to the Mojave Desert. One of the nation's prime wilderness recreation areas, the Sierra occupies a fifth of California and encompasses three national parks, eight national forests, and fifteen state parks.

WE HADN'T BEEN in our sleeping bags very long. The night outside was cold and uncommonly damp for late July in California's Sierra Nevada. A weather front had moved in from the northeast during the afternoon, pelting us with hail the size of mothballs. We had been on the edge of sleep, weary from hiking in the precipitous wilderness, our tents pitched on a wide granite ledge that was comfortably carpeted with pine needles.

Below us stretched Kerrick Meadow, on the north boundary of Yosemite National Park. There our string of ten burros dozed fretfully, occasionally shaking their heads and ringing the bells tied around their necks. We had left them near our portable "kitchen," surrounding the boxlike fiberglass panniers that held the food.

Dave Snyder, our trip leader, had suggested that tying the burros near the food might discourage unwanted visitors. That was important, because we were in bear country; Park Service signs had reminded us of the fact, and advised taking special precautions in storing food. Ideally, it should be hung from tree branches. But there was no way we could have put 20 heavy panniers out of the reach of bears. The burros were supposed to be our sentries.

I was nearly asleep when I first heard the noise, a sort of hollow thumping down by the little stream that meandered through the meadow. The thumping stopped, then resumed.

"Did you hear that?" I asked my wife, Alice.

"I think a burro is loose," she said. "We probably should go see."

Reluctant to leave my warm cocoon, I reached for my clothes, sneakers, and flashlight. We checked to be sure we had our police whistles. All of us carried them so we could signal if we became separated. While we dressed the din continued, but it stopped as we picked our way among granite boulders and descended to the meadow.

"It's *probably* a burro," I said to Alice. "But it could be something else. We'd better be careful."

Uneasily we probed with our flashlights. Every few seconds we shone them all around us. Near the cooking area we spotted three of the burros—Spooky, Fred, and usually noisy Hector, now quiet and apparently content. Among the rocks a shadow moved, a shadow darker than the others. Simultaneously Alice and I aimed our flashlights—and picked up two red, glowing eyes. We froze.

A bear!

Fragments of thoughts raced through my mind: Keep calm. Bears are basically fearful of people. Dave had said he once frightened one away just by making a lot of noise. Stay cool. Black bears often come into camp just looking for an easy meal.

*Breeeeeet . . . breeeeeet . . . breeeeeet!* went our whistles. Again the bear moved, a big black shape, then seemed to melt back into the shadows. Suddenly it turned to face us, and our light beams picked up its eyes once more. Was it going to charge?

"Get out of here! Scram, bear! Go away!" we shouted. To our relief, off it went, scrambling up the rocks to our left, past the area where most of our group had pitched their tents. Then, from almost the same direction as the bear had gone, we saw lights and heard Judy, Dave's wife and assistant trip leader.

"What is it?" she called.

"A bear."

"Where?"

"He headed your way."

Though Judy and the bear must have passed within yards of each other, she neither saw nor heard it. She joined us, followed by Dave and their 13-year-old daughter, Karen, and together we checked the area, at first finding nothing amiss. The burros seemed remarkably unconcerned, except for Spooky, who fidgeted a bit. The panniers had not been touched. As we spread out, shining our flashlights, Dave spotted the bear up among the boulders above us.

"Get out of here! Get out! Go away!" we chorused. The bear ambled off into the night.

On the stream bank we found our five-gallon billycan, a stout metal container with a tight-fitting lid. One corner had big holes in it—punctures made by sharp teeth. The lid had come off. The thumping noise had been the sound of the bear batting the billycan until it popped open. The food once inside was gone—a big hunk of cheese, some margarine, two half-pound bars of chocolate.

Our daughter, Alison, a second-year student at the University of Virginia, had stayed in the tent. Later I read the entry for that day in her journal:

"When I heard Mom and Dad say it was a bear, I started to tremble because I heard them call, 'He headed your way,' and I didn't know whom they were talking to."

Although the burros hadn't been very effective as sentinels, we moved several of them closer to the food, and we strung out ropes with bells before returning to our tents. We expected the bear would be back. It wasn't long before we heard the bells, and rushed out of our tents. More people came this time, including Alison. We set up a terrific racket.

Despite our precautions, the bear had managed this time to get past the burros, through the ropes, and at the panniers. He'd bitten into two large boxes of instant-potato flakes, leaving the results of a small blizzard on the ground. Evidently he didn't like them. Then he *(Continued on page 17)*

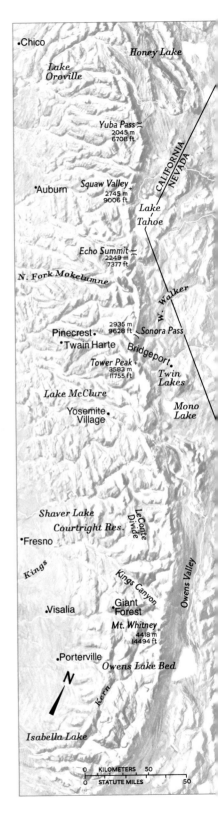

*Beginning a week-long trek, members of a Sierra Club burro pack trip—including the author and his family—follow a dusty trail across Leavitt Meadow. Below, a black bear looks out from a stand of pines. On two consecutive nights a bear raided the group's camp.*

Urged by 13-year-old Karen Snyder, Fred the burro enters Kerrick Meadow from the surrounding pine woods. Slung on his back, fiberglass panniers that packers call "kyacks" carry supplies; duffel bags hold personal gear. Below, weary hikers cast long shadows as they near a welcome campsite in late afternoon. Heavy travel has left the trail deeply rutted.

found something he did like—sweet powdered gelatin—and took a supply with him. Next morning we found a trail of empty gelatin boxes—raspberry here, orange there—and, last of all, a torn package of shredded coconut.

Determined to foil the bear (he was fast becoming The Bear in our minds), we stacked every pot and pan we had in precarious balance atop the panniers, and strung out more ropes with bells. Within an hour he was back. He came again, and again. Every time a pot would clatter or a bell would jangle, we would come out shouting—always with only temporary results.

Thus The Bear plagued us for two mostly sleepless nights. By the second night, however, we had become fairly blasé. We weren't getting much sleep, but then The Bear wasn't getting our food supplies. Alison wrote:

"After a while I ceased to be afraid that it would harm me—all it wanted was food. I think it also enjoyed getting us out of our bags and watching us blunder around in the dark like idiots."

KERRICK MEADOW was our chosen campsite for a two-day layover near the end of a week-long trip through the Sierra backcountry. There were 16 of us, and we were ready for a rest after a day in which we had walked more than 16 miles and crossed over a 9,900-foot-high pass.

It was my family's first acquaintance with the Sierra Nevada and what might be called true wilderness. We had decided on a burro pack trip (from among several more strenuous offerings of the Sierra Club Outing Department) because we thought it a reasonably easy way to get to know the terrain and to get used to the high elevations—7,000 feet and above—before a sortie into even higher, wilder country carrying our own backpacks.

We soon found, however, that there would be no easy introduction. No outing in this terrain is really easy, though nearly everything is rewarding. We also discovered that the help a burro provides by carrying one's supplies demands considerable repayment in time and attention.

I noticed that when we met backpackers on the trail, some would look down their noses as though we were traveling in luxury.

"Out for a stroll?" one asked sarcastically when he met us in the course of a steep climb.

Well, we did have some luxuries. But then we also had the burros. For things to work out, you have to like the animals, and not mind taking care of them. Fortunately, most of our group appreciated them. Alice, Alison, and I all had our favorites, and their donkeyish quirks and mournful, patient ways are etched in our hearts and memories.

*Pack trippers listen by the evening campfire as naturalist Dan Holmes reads a bit of Sierra lore. With the burros unpacked and curried, supper cooked and eaten, and pots and dishes washed, the campers can enjoy the fragrance of fire and forest and the enticing prospect of a snug sleeping bag.*

Near journey's end on the precipitous eastern side of the range, the party carefully makes a 1,200-foot descent. Short, steep zigzags interrupt the longer switchbacks on the narrow, rock-strewn trail. Opposite, Indian paintbrush displays its brilliant color amid granite boulders; from a rocky nook a marmot peers alertly; three fallen lodgepole pines entwine dead branches beside the path.

*Trailside sampler: golden-green corn lilies, a mountain yellow-legged frog. Forming flame-shaped leaves and three- to six-foot stalks, corn lilies grow in moist upland meadows and along stream banks. The frogs, because of the cold water and short Sierra summer, take two years to mature, spending the first winter as tadpoles under the ice. This frog swims in frigid, 9,600-foot-high Tower Lake. Some say the creatures smell like garlic.*

With my own companion, named Dammit, I established a wonderful rapport that was marred only when I wanted him to go and he didn't, or when I wanted him to stop and he wouldn't. One or the other happened with some frequency, and it took much effort and some forceful utterings of his name for me to prevail. But we shared some glorious sights.

We camped among lofty peaks that evoked Mark Twain's "convention of Nature's kings." We gazed with admiration as the first rays of eastern light played on barren, jagged ridges, and marveled in the evening at the last startling moments of alpenglow. We climbed the Sierra's rocky flanks, switchbacking up and down dizzying slopes, puffing and perspiring in the blinding light of midday, rejoicing in the sudden coolness and fragrance of piney woods. We trudged across ancient lake beds now become green meadows splashed with wild flowers. We drank from crystal streams and delighted in glacial lakes where trout leapt amid the upside-down reflections of shining peaks.

Within two weeks and a relatively few miles, we saw the seasons pass from the first stirrings of early spring to the heat of late summer. We studied trees and learned their names and habitats, and examined dozens of kinds of flowers. I looked for but failed to find water ouzels—amazing birds that swim and walk underwater and build nests of moss near waterfalls and tumbling brooks. I did see mountain yellow-legged frogs, animals that live in icy lakes above 7,000 feet. Reputedly they smell of garlic, but I can't confirm that—I resisted the impulse to pick one up.

As flatlanders from the East, we had been somewhat concerned about the elevations at which we would be hiking and the possibility of falling victim to altitude sickness. I had read many warnings of its effects: severe headaches and debilitating nausea. One way to avoid it, all agreed, was to become accustomed to the altitude gradually, and to take things easy at first. We decided to do just that, renting a small cabin at Kennedy Meadow in the Stanislaus National Forest at an elevation of 6,400 feet.

On the way into the Sierra, we stopped at the little resort village of Twain Harte, named for the two celebrated writers ("one of the pleasantest men I have ever known; also one of the unpleasantest," said Twain of the temperamental Bret Harte). Driving ever higher, we passed Pinecrest with its little lake and the Dardanelles with their conspicuous volcanic cones, then paused to admire the broken cliffs of hexagonal basaltic formations called the Columns of the Giants.

Our comfortable, rustic cabin stood at the edge of Kennedy Meadow and bordered a subterranean city populated by scurrying, ever-alert ground squirrels. For three days we took progressively longer hikes.

"Each day I like the mountains better," Alison wrote. "At first I saw them as hot and dusty. . . . The trails are still dusty, but the meadows are the greenest, lushest I've ever seen. It's amazing to me how one moment you can be climbing a rocky slope where trees are very sparse, and the next come upon one of these meadows."

Three times we saw mule deer. Twice they were 40 or 50 yards away, but once a big doe dashed silently across the trail just ahead of us. For the most part we saw few mammals—squirrels and chipmunks, a few marmots, a coyote.

Though we all puffed a bit at first, our lungs and leg muscles quickly gained strength, and we felt ready when we drove across 9,628-foot Sonora Pass on our way to meet the other pack trippers at Leavitt Meadow. Near the pass we came to a large patch of snow. We had seen plenty of it on distant peaks, but none this close. We piled out of the car to take pictures and throw snowballs at each other. I remembered Twain's reaction to summer snow in *Roughing It:*

"We were now far up toward the sky, and knew all the time that we must presently encounter lofty summits clad in the 'eternal snow' which was so commonplace a matter of mention in books, and yet when I did see it glittering in the sun on stately domes in the distance and knew the month was August . . . I was full as much amazed as if I never had heard of snow in August before."

LIKE OTHER Sierra passes to the north and south, Sonora Pass is a notch in the crest of the 400-mile-long mountain chain. The range itself is a massive, tilted block that slopes upward fairly gently from the west, then drops abruptly into the arid sagebrush country to the east. Our burro pack trip would begin just below the crest on its eastern side, and proceed along watercourses and over high saddles, through meadows and around lakes and ponds to Twin Lakes, near the town of Bridgeport, California. On the map it measured out to about 30 miles; on the ground it would be considerably more because of the switchbacks and wanderings of the trail. Except for a short incursion into Yosemite, our route would stay within the Toiyabe National Forest.

On a Saturday afternoon, we met our guides and companions for the next week at the campground near Leavitt Meadow. After supper and an orientation lecture from Dave on the basics of burro packing, we went to sleep under a star-filled sky. Up at four the next morning, some of us fetched the burros from their corral half a mile away and, after breakfast, packed each beast with its burden: first a packsaddle, a wooden frame from which a pannier was hung on each side; on top, duffel bags containing our clothing and equipment. The whole load was covered with canvas and tied down.

Each person was allowed 20 pounds of personal gear, and not an ounce more.

When most of the burros were laden, some of them decided on passive resistance. They lay down. Reaction was immediate and—since the animals did this often—soon became routine: shouts, pushing and prodding, tugs on the lead rope accompanied by more shouting, and if necessary, a procedure called "hop on Pop" that involved jouncing on the offending animal's shoulder or haunch. This was always successful, for our burros would not tolerate having anyone on them.

These animals work all summer, plodding through the Sierra. They are well cared for and, under a long-standing rental agreement, have been working for the Sierra Club for years. They come in two basic sizes—large and small—and their loads vary accordingly. Some have acquired fanciful names, some not so fanciful: Uncle Goofy, Triscuit, Hector, Ass. Though baleful of mien and cacophonic of voice, they are remarkably even-tempered, sturdy, and dependable. In the evenings, usually led by Hector, they would often serenade us with off-key bellowings and heavings.

FROM LEAVITT MEADOW we followed a trail along the West Walker River, still swollen by snowmelt. Our way led southward to Lane Lake, a small tarn surrounded by the weathered skeletons of dead pines—a ghost forest, probably the work of insects or the result of high water. Several of us went swimming in the cold lake, though not for long. But it was good to get cool and clean. The Sierra can be hot in summer and—especially if you're traveling near the end of a column of people and burros—very dusty.

After lunch we had the first steep climbing of the day, along the rocky gorge of the West Walker, always within hearing if not within sight of its torrent. It was an easy first day, and we camped in a stand of imposing Jeffrey pines.

Alice and I had signed up to cook that night and the next morning. Everyone would cook at least two meals during the trip. Our menu included canned ham, rice in ham gravy, dehydrated-and-reconstituted apple sauce, and raspberry gelatin chilled in the river. When there were no leftovers, we were quite pleased with our cooking skills. Later, of course, we realized that there never were any leftovers. Mountains make people hungry.

At 5 a.m. we were up again, cooking breakfast and packing the burros. Already we were growing familiar with what at first had seemed a hopelessly complicated way of tying down the loads. We used a squaw hitch, a tricky knot but—I was told—somewhat less complicated than the packer's traditional diamond hitch.

*Two forest monarchs dwarf a visitor to Atwell Grove in Sequoia National Park. At their feet, brackens extend fans of yard-long fronds. The famed giant sequoias, world's largest trees and among the oldest of living things, grow as natives only in the Sierra Nevada. Attaining heights of more than 300 feet and diameters of 30, the big trees live in scattered groves on the range's western slopes.*

There's another trick to packing a burro. When you're tightening the cinch of an experienced animal, it will usually take a deep breath, distending its belly and flanks. You may think you have the cinch tight, but after a while the burro will exhale, and the whole load will slip. The trick is to wait for your opponent to deflate, so to speak, and then to tighten the cinch quickly before the animal knows what you're about. A few exceptionally clever burros expect this, and will deflate only partially. You have to watch out for those.

Continuing along the West Walker, we followed the trail to Upper Piute Meadows, which gave us a long, green view with Hawksbeak and Ehrnbeck Peaks at the end of it. Then we began climbing in earnest to reach our next camp at about 9,200 feet. Above us loomed a fang-shaped pinnacle that, catching the afternoon light, shone like a beacon.

Next day was a layover day—time off for side trips, washing clothes, reading, resting. Most of us planned to climb to Tower Lake at the foot of Tower Peak. This would be our first excursion into true alpine country, the rocky, open zone above timberline.

The hike turned out as promised—an easy climb at first, then a steeper one, then a scramble at the end, so that we came upon the lake from below the rocky rim of its outlet. As

*Reflecting the azure sky, Cottonwood Creek ripples through a grassy meadow. Golden trout abound in the creek and the several lakes it connects. Below, state fish hatchery employees capture trout for a Sierra-wide program to stock lakes and streams. Native only to these mountains and honored as California's state fish, the golden trout thrives in backcountry waters above 8,000 feet.*

*Fishery worker deftly strips eggs from an anesthetized female golden trout; sperm already placed in the pan will fertilize the eggs. Pack mules will take the glistening harvest—nearly three-quarters of a million eggs—from the Cottonwood Lakes area to the Mount Whitney State Fish Hatchery. Fingerlings stock lakes throughout the Sierra, almost all of them dropped from airplanes. Opposite: Fish recover from sedation, used to keep them from struggling during the egg-collecting process.*

we hiked, naturalist Dan Holmes identified flowers and shrubs, among them western wallflower, mountain aster, columbine, both red and white mountain heather, and Labrador tea. At the edges of retreating snowfields we saw tender grass just beginning to sprout, the very start of spring—in July!—in this particular patch of mountainside.

On the way up, Alice and I stopped to rest within sight of a thundering waterfall. Everyone else kept going, and I was beginning to define a not very surprising natural law: Given an average hiking group of mixed ages, regardless of who starts where, by the end of the hike it will be sorted out so that the youngest are first and the oldest are last. We kept testing and proving this law. Alice and I were the oldest on the trip; invariably we were the last to arrive.

Tower Lake turned out to be a beauty, surrounded by mountains, snowfields, and the tumbled rocks of talus slopes. "Yesterday was super," Alison wrote. "The hike was rough, but interesting. . . . Tower Lake has a light green color around the edge which soon becomes a deep marine green. . . . I was quite surprised at its beauty, with its backdrop of tall peaks, and springy grass growing down to the water in places."

AFTER SUPPER that night, Dan read to us from the writings of the legendary Sierra mountaineer Norman Clyde, a man who loved this range and knew nearly every peak and valley. He was so drawn to the precipitous height called the North Palisade that he climbed it at least 35 times. Before his death in 1972, he was credited with 127 first ascents of Sierra peaks—far more than anyone else.

Clyde often carried a pack weighing more than 90 pounds; he had equipment for every mountain contingency, and some people declared he even carried an anvil, though Clyde denied this. At one with the mountains, he delighted in the ever-changing vistas, the solitude, the challenge.

The hike to Tower Lake had given me a glimmer of understanding of Clyde's love for the Sierra Nevada. Yet I must confess I was not born to write, as he did: "After a toilsome climb . . . up the rough abandoned trail over Harrison Pass at an elevation of 12,000 feet above the sea, I set down my heavy pack and looked about for a mountain to climb."

We had our own toilsome climb the next day when we broke camp and hiked to a high pass at the end of an interminable series of switchbacks. At the pass we stopped to refresh ourselves with snow from a shaded bank.

From here on, most of our traveling would be downhill, although—as in all mountains I have ever seen—we often had to go up to go down. We still had Buckeye Pass to master before entering Yosemite. But Buckeye turned out to be a gentle passage, sparsely treed and grassy and splashed with fields of faded blue phlox.

So far we had met few people on the trail—one mule packtrain and not more than a dozen backpackers. But we found plenty of signs that people had been there, evidence of hard use. It was not so much a question of litter—although we did find some—as a matter of wear and tear. At Buckeye Pass, for example, there isn't just a single trail; there are three sets of parallel ruts, worn down as people and animals abandon one path when it gets difficult and start another. The deepest ruts were cut almost 18 inches into the sod.

Camping areas take on a frayed, hard-packed appearance, too, and there are far too many fire-blackened stones. In large portions of the Sierra, especially the classified wilderness areas, officials require permits that limit numbers or regulate activity. Still, people keep coming. It seems a losing battle, no matter how careful and well-intentioned the visitors may be. They can't go through the wilderness walking on air, and every contact between the human foot and the soil is another small defeat for the soil. This is particularly true in the High Sierra, where the soil is often thin and where it may take a pine seedling 35 years to grow a foot tall.

Buckeye Pass took us into Yosemite's Kerrick Meadow, where we would gratefully spend two days before resuming our trek out of the mountains. This had been our long, 16-mile day; and I don't believe anyone remembers much of the evening beyond setting up camp and crawling into sleeping bags. If The Bear came that night, no one noticed. It wasn't until the next evening that the alarms began.

Kerrick Meadow is a scant five-minute walk from rock-rimmed Peeler Lake, a glacier-gouged bowl of deep, clear water perched on a ridge. At times of high levels from snow-melt, it has two outlets, one to the west, one to the northeast.

"The approach from Kerrick Meadow was graced by an unconcerned doe browsing near a loop in the trail," my wife, Alice, wrote in her diary. "The scene was unexpectedly beautiful. A glade surrounds pools spilling one to another in small, swift waterfalls that mark the beginning of Rancheria Creek. Nature's arrangement would evoke the envy of any landscape architect. Standing on the granite shore, I watched the sky change from heavy gray to radiant rose, with the alpenglow reflected on the lake's surface and intensified by the crystals in the surrounding rocks. As the colors faded and the mountains began to slip into night shadow, I realized that I had been given a special treat."

The trip out of the mountains took us along the shore of Peeler Lake on a rainy morning. The trail, traversing solid rock, at times became a ledge so narrow that the burros' panniers almost scraped against the (Continued on page 32)

FOLLOWING PAGES:
*Lingering snow clings to a wind-scoured mountain crest and helps define the slender line of the Mount Whitney Trail. At far right, a 14,015-foot peak memorializes John Muir, naturalist and conservationist, one of the Sierra's early explorers and probably its most eloquent admirer.*

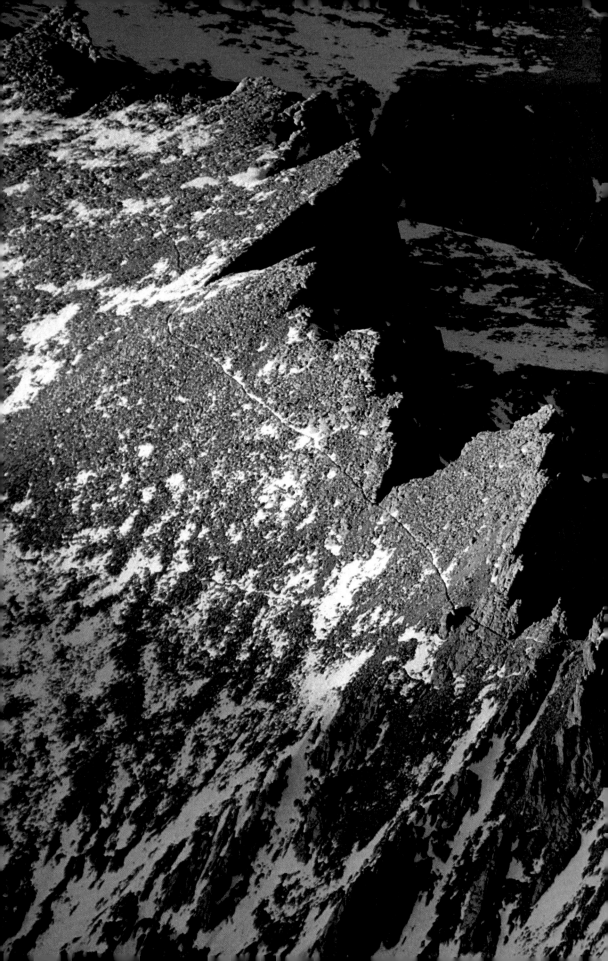

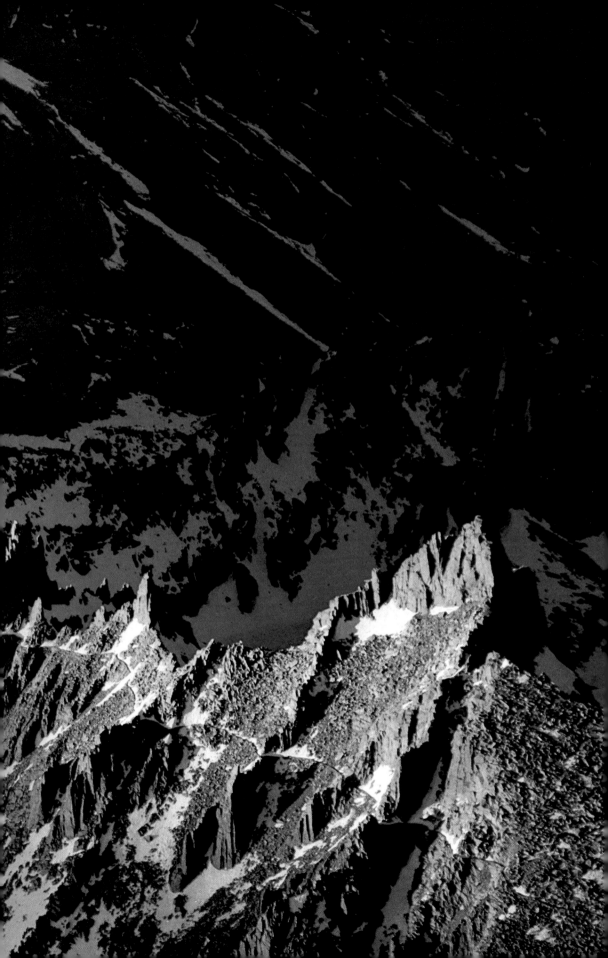

Shawl of sparkling foam covers a mountain's rocky shoulder at
Tokopah Falls, Sequoia National Park, below a granite spire called
the Watch Tower. At left, school principal Jim Parks of Hanford,
California, casts for trout, accompanied by Tawny, an orphaned
mule deer fawn cared for since infancy by Parks and his students.
At upper left, a rainbow trout takes Jim's line in the turbulent waters
of the East Fork of the Kaweah River.

mountainside. Beyond the lake we made a long, serpentine descent, and at the bottom skirted a field of corn lilies, their bright green leaves scattered with large raindrops that gleamed like translucent pearls.

To Alison, this last day of the pack trip was the best. "The rocks and boulders were amazing," she wrote. "We passed by one cliff where a huge piece of granite had dropped off, leaving a long, smooth scar, as though someone had cut it with a saw. All the rocks were tinted by lichens—some green, some black, some gray. At one place there was a mountain of rock ahead of us that looked like some magical city in a fantasy book, perhaps an artist's conception of where a hobbit or a gnome might dwell. The mountain was made up of little domes, one atop another. The mist and lichens added to the effect."

Returning to reality, she made the laconic entry: "The switchbacks were very steep downhill."

Steep they were, and at the bottom of another long series we came to a tumbling waterfall where, for a few fleeting moments, we wrestled with tragedy.

The first burro into the stream slipped and fell. It was Ass, sweet-tempered, reliable Ass. The force of the current carried her to the edge of the waterfall, where a fallen tree prevented her from going over the edge. She was on her side, apparently unable to get up, and we feared a broken leg.

Dave, Judy, and Karen jumped into the water, which came above their knees, and quickly removed the duffel bags and panniers. We shouted and prodded, but Ass was a dead weight and made no effort to rise. She lay stiff in the icy water, rolling her eyes in terror so that the whites showed. Somehow we dragged her to the edge of the stream, worked a rope behind her haunches, and pulled her rear end upright. Ass then rose on her front legs and finally staggered out of the water. She had no serious injury and was only slightly bruised by the rocks. She shivered and shook while we rubbed her dry, but soon recovered enough to eat several pieces of hard candy.

Judy and Dave raise and work burros on their Carrollton, Ohio, farm, and I asked Judy why Ass had been so passive and uncooperative. "Sometimes, when they get in trouble, they just seem to give up," she said. "They won't do anything to help themselves."

We were apprehensive as we approached another ford in the stream, but Ass took it in stride, her fall perhaps already forgotten.

Now the burros seemed to know we were nearing the end of the pack journey, and there was no holding them back. Soon we were at Twin Lakes, saying our goodbyes and giving the animals their last candy treats. We drove off to

Bridgeport, where our priorities were clear: showers, laundry, dinner, and bed.

Next morning we headed for Mono Lake, a large body of salt water that is—or was—the nesting site of perhaps a quarter of the world's population of California gulls. We had seen these graceful birds soaring over Peeler and other High Sierra lakes, and they seemed incongruous so far from the ocean. At Mono they feed on the lake's teeming population of brine shrimp. Until recently they had an enormous rookery on Negit Island.

Because much of Mono's inflow of fresh water has been diverted to supply Los Angeles, 275 miles away, the lake's level has dropped 45 feet since 1941. This has exposed a land bridge between Negit Island and the shore. In 1979, predators overran the rookery, killing many of the chicks and causing three-fourths of the lake's breeding population—about 46,700 birds in 1978—to abandon nesting efforts.

The diversion of water that would sustain Mono Lake is a matter of heated controversy. A citizens' committee has been formed to try to save the lake. And there are people in Bridgeport who will tell you Los Angeles doesn't even need Mono's water—that the metropolis wastes almost as much as it obtains from Mono Lake tributaries.

O NCE MORE we drove into the Sierra, going over Tioga Pass and into the magnificent Yosemite Valley. The landscape looked different here—more heroic in proportion, more granitic, much more heavily traveled. Nevertheless, on one temporarily deserted road we saw a coyote purposefully crossing the pavement with "that long, calm, soft-footed trot," as Mark Twain aptly wrote.

Alice had to return to the East. Alison and I left her at the Fresno airport and, already surfeited with the life of motels and restaurants, headed back to the wilderness.

Our guide for the next week would be Tom Hunt of Palo Alto who, with his friend Robert (Van) Adams, had produced a book on the old emigrant trails to California. Tom knows the Sierra well, and had promised me a backpacking week that would not be "too strenuous" but would take us through some spectacular country. I should have known. Tom was absolutely right about the last part, but I could argue about the first.

Van would be coming with us, as would his stepson, Josh Hatch, who was wearing a cast up to his elbow from a roller-skating accident, and Josh's friend Dan Plummer. We met them at Shaver Lake, and drove on to our trailhead at Courtright Reservoir. The reservoir was a huge dry mudhole, emptied of its water to permit improvements to the hydroelectric generating station.

*Positioned by glacier power, a four-foot-wide boulder rests on an expanse of granite in Yosemite National Park. Left behind as glaciers melted 10,000 years ago or more, such boulders comprised part of the immense load of debris carried by the moving ice. Opposite: A western tiger swallowtail butterfly flutters above a mountain stream.*

With most of the afternoon still ahead of us, we decided to start hiking immediately. After several hours we reached the eastern flank of Maxson Dome and set up camp near a small brook. The next day was hot and uneventful. We plodded on sandy, rutted trails through meadows and heavily scented pine woods. The unaccustomed weight of the backpack slowed me down, and I was happy when we stopped for the day on the North Fork of the Kings River, whose swift waters rushed over a glacier-polished bed of granite. Quiet backwater pools gave us a chance to swim and wash off the dust of the trail.

In her journal, Alison wrote:

"I think this is the most beautiful river I've ever seen. It is so different. The water glides over sheets of rolling granite. There are dozens of chutes and slides."

We retired early that night. Before falling asleep, I reflected on the relative merits of backpacking and burro packing. As backpackers we had more freedom; we could camp wherever we chose without worrying about the animals' needs. We felt more self-sufficient, and somehow closer to the wilderness. On the negative side, there would be no luxury meals, only lightweight food easily carried. And we had our heavy packs, with sleeping bags and tents, to lug around. Which mode of travel is more satisfying, I decided, depends on one's objectives.

As expected, the hike was rough all the next day. We climbed more than 2,000 feet, almost to timberline. Tom kept promising us flat stretches ahead, but they always seemed just as tilted as the rest of the landscape. When we finally reached McGuire Lake, I was ready to quit for the day, but Tom kept us moving. Both McGuire and the lower lake into which it flows are gradually filling with silt and sand, and grass is invading their shorelines. Eventually the silting will be complete, and the lake beds will turn into meadows. Then trees may encroach upon the grassland, and the meadows gradually become forests. Hiking through the Sierra, one can see examples of every stage of this process.

For two nights we camped at Guest Lake at the foot of Blackcap Mountain. The elevation was 10,160 feet; until we turned homeward at the end of the week, we would not be below 10,000 feet. The lakes in this area were well stocked with trout, and Josh and Dan caught enough to add a welcome supplement to our diet of noodles and soup.

On one side trip from Guest Lake, Alison's head reached 12,000 feet even if her feet did not. That was the day she, Tom, Van, and the boys climbed 11,998-foot Mount Hutton. "On one side of our peak," she wrote, "all the mountains were in varying shades of brown and seemed to consist of dirt. On the other sides, the mountains were made

*Laden with blossoms, tall stalks of yucca plants reach toward the sun above the Middle Fork of the Kaweah River. Massive Castle Rocks hide behind morning haze in the distance.*
*The Sierra spring brings forth a myriad of blooms and the pervasive sound of torrents fed by melting snow. Above, visitors aim their cameras near Tokopah Falls.*

*Etched in light and shadow, the Sierra's stern vistas conceal a welcoming gift reserved for the perceptive hiker: an unforgettable experience of wilderness, of sights and sounds and smells a world apart from normal daily concerns.*

of dark gray granite. They were all jagged, whereas the brown mountains were smooth. . . . Some of the rocks near the edge were arranged like a throne, and I felt rather like one of the gods on Mount Olympus—that is, until I looked down, and then I felt very small. Mountains like Hutton seem so very powerful when one climbs them."

I didn't climb Mount Hutton, but stayed behind to enjoy the scenery by myself. I left the group above Schoolmarm Lake, somewhere around 11,200 feet. They went down into a shallow valley and up the other side. I walked back toward the lake over the trackless expanse of shattered granite. Overhead, the sky was a pristine blue. To the west I could just make out the outline of the Coast Ranges. To the east and northeast rose the massive crest of the LeConte Divide. Below, a chain of lakes flowed one into the next—Bullet, Holster, Wah Hoo, Six Shooter, Schoolmarm, Crabtree. Their varying depths and locations made them a palette of blues and greens.

Aside from a few grasses, alpine flowers, and stunted whitebark pines, there wasn't another living thing in sight. Ah, solitude! I thought joyfully as I slipped into the chilly lake. But solitude is almost never absolute in this modern world; within minutes I heard the roar of jet engines, and directly overhead passed an airliner full of people intent on private errands. Where, I asked myself, can one be truly alone?

FROM GUEST LAKE we moved our camp to Horsehead, another "hanging lake" whose outlet cascades down a rocky incline. It provided a fitting setting for our last night in the high country, with its massive backdrop of granite ramparts and a classic cirque—glacier-carved rock amphitheater—that could have illustrated a geology textbook.

Next morning we headed cross-country to pick up our old trail near the rushing torrent of Fall Creek. In another day we made it back to Courtright Reservoir, though I was lagging far behind and Alison stayed back with me. Both of us were tired after two weeks in the mountains, hungry for real food, aching for hot showers and clean, soft beds.

But we had acquired an understanding and respect for the magic Sierra Nevada. We had experienced and appreciated its grandeur, its remoteness, its crisp, clear air, its clean, sweet water. Every step had been worth the effort.

When, with dragging feet, Alison and I approached Courtright Reservoir, Van saw us from a couple of hundred yards away. He drove over and offered us a ride to our car.

"No," I said. "Thanks just the same."

I'd been carrying that backpack for a week. And, by golly, I was going to carry it back to where I'd started. Last guys have their pride.

# The Cascade Range

*Born of volcanic fire, shaped by glacial ice, serrated peaks of the Goat Rocks break through*

*By* H. ROBERT MORRISON
*Photographed by* FARRELL GREHAN

*a bank of ragged clouds in the Cascades of southern Washington.*

*Reaching from California northward into British Columbia, the Cascade Range dominates the geography of the Pacific Northwest and divides it into semiarid inland and damp coastal provinces. The range presumably took its name from the Columbia River's cascades, inundated in 1937 by Bonneville Dam. National parks now protect 1.2 million acres of these spectacular mountains; the Forest Service administers most of the rest—about 14 million acres. In the spring of 1980, underscoring the Cascades' volcanic origins, Mount St. Helens erupted after more than a century of silence.*

THE SOFT CRUNCH under my snowshoes settled into a satisfying rhythm as I followed the switchbacks of a mountain road in the Cascade Range near Easton, Washington. The crisp spring air was bracing, and the sounds of traffic on Interstate Highway 90 off to the south had dwindled to a distant murmur. Ahead of me strode Gene Prater, farmer, renowned mountaineer, and author of a book on snowshoeing. I was just beginning to get a feel for this unfamiliar mode of travel when Gene veered toward the edge of the road and a 15-foot-high snowbank. As I watched, he climbed straight up. At the top he rested on his ice ax.

"Come on," he called. "What are you waiting for? Nothing to it." He smiled. "The snow is good and solid. Just kick the toe of your snowshoe straight in and step up."

I drove my right snowshoe into the bank to my instep, and gingerly tested my weight. The snow seemed solid enough. Moments later I stood beside Gene, happy to admit that climbing the snowbank was much easier than it looked.

This was my first visit to the Cascades, a volcanic range running from south of Lassen Peak in California to the junction of the Fraser and Thompson Rivers in British Columbia. Ten mighty snowclad volcanoes rise above the jagged, glacier-carved ridges that build to a jumbled climax in the rugged North Cascades. Together the Cascades hold more glacial ice than all other mountains in the United States combined, except for those in Alaska. I was to spend two and a half months exploring the Cascade Range, first on this visit in early spring and again in the summer. I crisscrossed the mountains by car from Washington south to California; and I backpacked nearly a hundred miles, mostly through wilderness.

But on this April day I was still a novice, and unprepared for the rewards awaiting us when we reached the top of Amabilis Mountain. The views immediately made all the effort of climbing worthwhile. To the southwest, Mount Adams's bulky outline rode above the intervening ridges like a ship under sail. Closer and more westerly rose massive Mount Rainier, an apparition above a low bank of clouds. Northward, to the left of Mount Daniel, I could glimpse Chimney Rock now and again as haze cleared for a moment before closing back in. To the northeast was Mount Stuart.

Two thousand feet below us lay icebound Kachess and Keechelus Lakes. With the practical eye of a farmer, Gene appraised their shorelines and hoped there would be enough water to irrigate the broad fields of the Yakima and Kittitas Valleys through the dry summer season.

On the way down, Gene headed for every steep slope he could find, gliding as gracefully as a skier. I tried repeatedly, always with the same result: I ended on my backside, leaving three tracks instead of two, and consequently rode home in wet trousers. As we discussed the climb in Gene's homey kitchen near Ellensburg, his wife, Yvonne, asked how I had done. "I think," Gene responded, "that Bob has mastered the sitting glissade!"

A few days later Yvonne, herself a journalist, took me to meet one of her favorite friends. We parked in the driveway of Mabel Abrahamson's place west of Ellensburg and walked across the pasture beside her house. Mabel, a short, slightly stooped woman, was wearing mud-spattered overalls and a light jacket over a blouse with a colorful pattern. A straw hat shaded her eyes, bright and lively behind thick glasses. Lines of upturned wet sod, rich brown against the green grass, bordered the shallow irrigation ditch she was clearing. As we approached, she rested on her shovel. The former dairy ranch is now a quiet tree farm, but she still finds plenty of hard work to do.

Mabel was born in England in 1896, and four years later emigrated to Alberta with her parents. She moved to Washington in the 1920s and worked as a cook for crews harvesting wheat with horse-drawn combines. There she met and married Oscar Abrahamson, who had bought the ranch on Manastash Creek where Mabel still lives. Oscar built a barn, hewing its beams by hand, and they raised a herd of Holsteins.

One source of ready cash was the bakery in Ellensburg. Every week Oscar and Mabel cut, split, and delivered two cords of wood to fuel its ovens. And they fought the rattlesnakes that slithered across the road from the rocky canyon walls. "I didn't like to kill them," Mabel said. "I think it's cruel to have to kill an animal that's warning you it's there. But they were a danger to our animals, as well as to us."

We walked toward the front of her house, where fruit trees blossomed in the sun. But the day was too beautiful to go inside, and Mabel suggested we sit on short logs from the woodpile while we had some lemonade. As I turned to get the logs, Mabel cautioned, "Be sure to roll them away from the pile before you pick them up. Sometimes rattlesnakes hide in there."

I was very careful to follow her advice.

Mabel's love of this mountain land and its living things was a theme she returned to again and again. The soaring flight of a pair of hawks that nested just across the creek; the bright green of early spring leaves; the majesty of ice-capped peaks—all are still a source of wonder and delight to Mabel.

Jack Kirsch, too, has been drawn irresistibly to the mountains. He freely admits to gold fever, and for him it's a terminal case. One afternoon Yvonne and I visited Jack— "last of the pick-and-shovel miners," he said—in the village of Liberty north of Ellensburg.

Today a handful of cabins and house trailers along

Low mists linger above the rapids of a stream in the Mount Baker National Forest. Here—and all along the western side of the Cascades—grow lush groves of mixed conifers, nourished by precipitation that may reach 80 inches a year. Elsewhere in the national forest, thick moss (above) greens a tangle of vine maples; blossoming skunk cabbages (below) herald the arrival of spring.

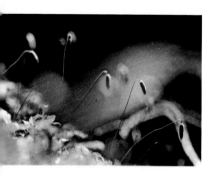

*Diminutive plants called sporophytes nod above a mat of moss near Mount Baker in northern Washington. Opposite, a wood violet grows near Stevens Pass. One of the most widely seen violets of the Pacific Northwest, the flower also bears the common name Johnny-jump-up.*

Williams Creek, Liberty suggests only a shadow of yesteryear. Although an Army lieutenant named George B. McClellan had reported traces of gold in Kittitas Valley as early as 1853, the first major discovery in the district came by accident one evening in the autumn of 1873. A party of prospectors made an early camp along Swauk Creek, according to one account, so they could boil their lice-infested clothes. One of them went down to the creek for water, overturned a rock, and spied a nugget. Popping it into his mouth, he picked up a bucket in each hand and ran back to camp. His companions thought a bear was after him until he put down the buckets and opened his mouth. Within an hour the men had panned five dollars' worth of gold dust and found another nugget worth a hundred dollars.

Word of the strike spread slowly, but in time miners began flocking to the area. By the late 1890s a gold camp called Liberty, then on Swauk Creek, and Meaghersville, on Williams Creek, were both well-established towns. Many of the miners had brought their families to live with them, and they never tolerated the lawlessness and carousing associated with most other mining camps. Residents became involved in community life; they established literary and debating societies; and church suppers and genteel dancing parties regularly drew visitors from larger, older Ellensburg.

The gold itself proved extremely unpredictable. It occurred here and there in placer deposits and isolated hard-rock lodes. When the mining companies had thoroughly dredged the creeks, large-scale operations became unprofitable. Occasionally some miner would find a placer worth several thousand dollars and inspire another flurry of activity. But by 1916 old Liberty was abandoned, and its store and post office were moved to Meaghersville. The handful of families remaining there renamed that village Liberty.

Today Jack Kirsch and a few others mine small claims and rework the old tailings and dumps of the Swauk district. A tall, lean man with dark-rimmed glasses, Jack was wearing a plaid flannel shirt and bib overalls as he loosened the rocky earth with a pick and shoveled it into a homemade sluice box. A canvas hose directed a stream of water into the top end of the box. Riffles of coarse screen laid over carpet in the bottom would catch the heavy gold dust as it settled.

"I'm moving these tailings to reach a shear line they cover," Jack told me as he worked. "There's a good possibility I'll find a pocket of gold there. Meanwhile, this sluicing is just for whatever dust I can get."

Jack labored for an hour or so in the warm sun, then cleaned out his sluice. He lifted the strips of screen and carpet from the bottom of the box and sloshed them up and down in a large plastic bucket. After he poured off most of the water, I looked into the bucket. All I could see was mud.

Back at his cabin he began to work the mud, dipping his gold pan into a drum of water and deftly swirling it around with the ease of fifty years' experience. Minutes later he held up the pan. Sparkling against the dark background was the glitter of yellow dust. I didn't have to ask him how he caught gold fever; I came close to being infected myself.

That afternoon as we sat in Jack's library—one room of an old log cabin he bought and moved next to his home, and now overflowing with books and periodicals—he told me he was born in 1900 and had lived in Liberty since 1928. He has worked as a hunter and trapper in Alaska, as a laborer on various railroads, and as a stonecutter. "I'd work till I saved a grubstake," he said, "and then I'd work harder as a prospector using up the money than I did earning it."

I found Jack a man of varied talents and a wide range of interests. When I asked what he does when snow covers his claims, he said simply, "I read and study, and I listen to records and the radio." Mostly he reads philosophy, but his hobby is astrology. His dozens of opera records are worn and scratchy from being played repeatedly on a battered portable phonograph, so now he listens to opera broadcasts as often as possible. His favorite composer is Wagner; because mine is Verdi, we had a friendly argument concerning the relative merits of German and Italian operas.

FOLLOWING PAGES: *Their growth stunted by long, harsh winters and fleeting summers, subalpine firs and whitebark pines struggle for life among fallen companions in Mount Rainier National Park. In the distance beyond the White River looms 14,410-foot Mount Rainier, mightiest of the Cascades and, in these parts, often called simply "The Mountain."*

FROM ELLENSBURG I drove north to Chelan, caught the passenger ferry *Lady of the Lake* to Lucerne on upper Lake Chelan, and boarded a bus for the ten-mile ride to Holden. This unusual religious community was once an active copper-mining center; but in 1957 declining yields closed it down, and Holden became briefly a ghost town.

In 1960, at the request of a farsighted Lutheran layman, the mining company gave the townsite to a nonprofit Lutheran corporation. With the help of volunteers, the buildings were renovated, and today the village serves as a year-round retreat center. Guests—as many as 400 a week in summer—attend lectures and craft classes, discuss religious and social issues, and go fishing or hiking in the heart of the Cascades.

I was struck by the sense of close community I felt at Holden. "Most people who join the staff here are at a turning point in their lives," business manager Werner Janssen told me. "They find at Holden an atmosphere that offers time for individual meditation and development and the support of a concerned group of Christians."

My fiancée, Meredith Wollenberg, joined me for two backpacking trips into the Cascades. The first began at Holden, and crossed the Glacier Peak Wilderness.

Jim Smith, an electrician *(Continued on page 50)*

*Deadhorse Creek tumbles
down a bed of polished
lava boulders in Mount
Rainier National Park. With
spring snowmelt flowers
appear, attracting wasp-like
syrphid flies. At left,
short hairs cover the sepals
of western pasqueflowers;
lupines (center) emit
a rich perfume; a syrphid fly
clings to a red penstemon.
Below, pink spring beauties
open at sunrise; avalanche
lilies nod in the breeze.*

*Solitary pine east of White Pass in Washington attests to the rigors of its existence. Heavy snows have bent its branches; but most Pacific storms never cross the Cascade crest, and the vegetation of the eastern slopes reflects the drier climate. Above, a ladybug rests on spring foliage bursting from an oak branch; an arrow-leafed balsamroot lifts its showy flower.*

on the Holden staff, accompanied Meredith and me as we left the village early one morning in July. Jim, an enthusiastic mountain climber, would guide us to Lyman Lake nearly eight miles away. "The lake is beautiful," he told us, "and it has good campsites. But if I were you, I'd plan to spend the night beyond it, near Cloudy Pass. This is the season for deer flies, and Lyman Lake usually is thick with them."

He was right. The flies appeared in swarms, and obviously took our presence as an invitation to lunch. Jim quickly said goodbye and hurried back to Holden.

Meredith and I rested a few minutes longer. We weren't yet acclimated to the 5,500-foot elevation, and the last mile of trail leading up to Lyman Lake rose in a series of steep switchbacks. The annoying insects soon prompted us to move on, but before shouldering our packs, we walked to the shore for a last look.

Suddenly Meredith pointed. On an islet perhaps 20 yards from shore stood a doe. Hesitantly she moved toward us, followed by two spotted fawns. When she saw us she froze, ears alert, and the fawns did the same. For an unforgettable moment they stood still; then the doe bounded off to our right with one of the fawns close behind. The other, more curious, continued to stare at us. Then, realizing how far away its mother was, the fawn splashed after her, its awkward legs barely reaching to the bottom of the shallow lake.

We camped that night in a small grove of alpine fir just below Cloudy Pass. All about us the vivid vermilion of Indian paintbrush punctuated highland meadows blue with lupines. Above the carpet rose the hairy puffs of pasque-flowers already gone to seed, like dish mops stuck handle-first into the thin soil. Beside the stream where we drew our drinking water nodded a columbine, its showy scarlet-and-yellow flowers each a study in perfection.

The next morning we climbed to 6,478-foot Cloudy Pass, where Boy Scouts bound for Lyman Lake were having a snowball fight beside the trail. Beyond the pass we skirted the South Fork of Agnes Creek, then climbed again to Suiattle Pass. Ahead loomed the majestic bulk of Glacier Peak. Its ice-white summit sparkled against a nearly cloudless sky of deep blue. Almost half a mile below us thundered the Suiattle River, its waters milky with glacial dust, its roar clearly audible even at that distance.

When we reached Image Lake that afternoon we were fortunate to find a campsite. So well known has this gem of a mountain lake become that its very popularity has endangered it; alpine meadows are far too fragile for crowds. So the U. S. Forest Service has limited the number of campsites here, and placed them a quarter mile from the shores.

As the sun dipped toward the horizon, banks of clouds

*Crater Lake, at 1,932 feet the deepest in the United States, fills the caldera of a once-mighty volcano in southern Oregon. Some 6,600 years ago, explosive eruptions spewed forth lava and spread ashes over an area of 350,000 square miles. The cone, unable to support its own weight, then collapsed inward. Much more recent volcanic activity within the caldera produced Wizard Island, a cinder cone named for its fancied resemblance to a sorcerer's hat.*

gathered in the valley far below us. Shades of pink, steadily deepening to crimson, invaded the sky; the ice and snow-fields of Glacier Peak caught the colors and glowed. Along with three other backpackers camped nearby, Meredith and I stood transfixed. Although we were shivering, we could not pull ourselves away from the spectacle until darkness fell. Even then, the top of Glacier Peak remained visible, its 10,541-foot summit catching the final sunlight after the lesser peaks around it lay bathed in shadow.

We had just crawled into our sleeping bags when we heard music. Meredith abruptly sat up. "Who would bring a radio to such a lovely, isolated spot?" she demanded in indignation. I listened for a moment. "It's a harmonica," I said. Our fellow backpacker soon ended his serenade with "Home, Sweet Home," and from the nearby tents a round of spontaneous applause rang through the darkness.

Next morning we began our descent toward the Suiattle River. Back and forth the trail folded; I counted 32 switchbacks before we reached a comparatively level stretch. Hiking downhill requires less stamina than climbing, but it tests muscles unexercised by walking uphill or on level ground. By the time we reached our campsite at Canyon Creek, we had descended nearly 4,000 feet, most of it in the first five miles. Just to lie on the ground with our feet and legs propped on a log was blissful.

By contrast the next day's hike was an easy stroll, and Meredith and I arrived early at the roadhead that marked the terminus of our high-country adventure together. By coincidence it was near the same town—Marblemount—where a few weeks before I had met logger Harry Martin.

L OGGING IS A MAJOR industry in the Cascades, and I wanted to watch loggers at their jobs. I arranged to meet Harry Martin an hour after his men began work.

"You can't keep banker's hours if you're going to learn anything about logging." The shout boomed out from the barnlike garage and maintenance shop in Marblemount where Harry repairs his vehicles. As I walked toward the doorway, Lawrence K. Buchanan—known since childhood by his nickname "Weasel"—appeared. Grease stained his coveralls, and a battered hard hat perched at an angle above his grizzled face. "Shame on you," he continued. "It's already five o'clock!"

Harry Martin grinned. "Don't let Weasel bother you. To tell you the truth, I didn't mind starting at five this morning. It gave me an extra hour's sleep."

A wiry man of 62 without a trace of gray in his straight black hair, Harry stood beside his green pickup truck and gave some final instructions to his employees. He wore a red-and-black plaid shirt; suspenders—badge of the logger—held up his work pants. We climbed into the pickup and Harry drove to the logging site in the Mount Baker National Forest near Darrington.

The whine of chain saws echoed through the trees as we clambered down a steep slope. During a pause in the noise, Harry alerted the fallers—the men who fell the trees—with a loud "Hello!" Turning to me, he said, "I don't want to surprise them while they're cutting. It's dangerous work."

Bob Anderson and his assistant, Ron Medford, greeted us; Bob moved to the base of a tree and peered upward. I asked what he was looking for.

"I'm checking to see how the tree is leaning, and where the heaviest limbs are," he replied. "Then I'll know how to cut it so it falls where I want it." He pointed. "I'm going to lay it down right there."

Starting his saw, he cut a foot-deep notch in the trunk, facing the direction of fall. Then he began cutting on the opposite side. When his saw was partway in, he shouted to Ron, who picked up a wedge and drove it into the cut behind Bob's saw. Moments later the tree crashed down—right where Bob had indicated.

Immediately Ron climbed onto the trunk. Attaching one

end of a tape measure to the cut end, he measured off the lengths specified by the mill and marked each with a slash sawed into the bark, trimming off limbs as he went. Then he began cutting the trunk into lengths.

As I watched one after another of the great trees being cut down, my feelings were jumbled. I knew the huge clearing would remain a scar on the mountainside for at least ten years. Initially, at least, the soil would lie vulnerable to increased erosion. On the other hand, lumber is obviously an important factor in the soaring cost of new home construction. For those in need of housing, an increase in the harvesting of trees might help to steady home prices. Furthermore, the Douglas fir—the primary timber crop here—grows best in the full sunlight of clearcut areas. Obviously logging raises many-sided issues.

Farther down the mountain, Harry showed me another aspect of logging. At this site the fallers had completed cutting. Now a crew of men worked to move the felled timber to the logging road where it would be loaded onto trucks. A "spar tree"—a tall fir topped and stripped of its branches—stood beside the road. "Once all logging was done this way," Harry said. "Now most outfits use steel towers. Not many men even know how to rig a spar tree anymore."

Simply stated, the spar tree's purpose is to support and anchor a system of cables and pulleys so the yarder engineer can haul in logs from a wide area of mountainside to a level loading site. Since the riggers were often out of sight of the yarder engineer, the boss of the rigging crew—the hook tender—carried a small radio transmitter, or "talkie-tooter," that blew the yarder whistle by remote control. A code of long and short blasts told everyone which cables would be taut and slack, and which way they could move.

Through binoculars I watched the rigging crew. They would catch a pair of dangling cables, or chokers; fasten each around a log; then retreat as the cables tugged the logs free and dragged them to the loading area. The men moved swiftly about the slippery tangle of felled trees, as graceful and surefooted as ballet dancers.

"These boys take pride in their work," Harry told me. "You don't find many like that."

JUST A FEW MILES west of Marblemount, at Rockport, I met another man who takes pride in his work. His name is Ken Bostard, and he makes musical instruments.

I first talked with Ken, a tall, thin man with graying black hair and a neat beard, on a gloomy afternoon in early spring. Snowbanks lined the North Cascades Highway, and the entrance to nearby Rockport State Park had not yet been plowed. We sat in the immaculate workshop Ken had built

*Gulls wheel and soar above the marshy shores of Lower Klamath National Wildlife Refuge on the Oregon-California border. In the distance rises snowclad Mount Shasta, 14,162 feet high.*

and where he was living until his house was completed. I asked him what had brought him to the Cascades.

"I once held a very good job in the electronics industry in Los Angeles," he said, "but I didn't get much personal satisfaction from my work. In 1972 I finally quit and moved to Seattle.

"I have always enjoyed working with my hands, doing something creative. After I got involved with woodworking, a friend suggested I try making musical instruments. My first attempt was a dulcimer; gradually I built more complicated instruments, and they turned out well.

"Meanwhile, I heard of this land for sale. It offered an ideal combination; it is secluded, yet only 2½ hours' drive from Seattle. And it's in the mountains. Some friends and I went together and bought the property.

"By this time I had begun to specialize, making harps and Middle Eastern instruments. Since I'm self-employed, I don't have to work in town. So here I am."

Most of Ken's creations have been sold. When I asked to see an example of a Middle Eastern oud, he brought forth a lute-like instrument somewhat larger than a mandolin, with a deeply curved back. I was amazed at how little it weighed. "I really find the instruments fascinating," Ken said. "But now I'm spending most of my time working on my house."

55

*American avocet wings above Lower Klamath Lake, one of five national wildlife refuges in the Klamath Basin south of Crater Lake. Located on the busy migration route called the Pacific Flyway, the Klamath refuges provide food and resting places for as many as four million birds at a time. Some water birds, especially pelicans and cormorants, nest here. At left, a cormorant dries its wing feathers. Below, a formation of white pelicans brakes to a landing. These social birds usually fly in groups and often beat their wings in unison. An observer of their aerobatics, Oregon naturalist William L. Finley, described one swooping maneuver: "They used the sky as a big toboggan-slide...."*

*Checking timber for growth, forestry technician Robin Du Brin calculates the height of a tree in the Mount Baker National Forest near Rockport, Washington. Her report will help the Forest Service determine the optimum time for thinning the stand.*

Together we inspected the unfinished shell of the home he had designed. It was the shape of a hexagon, and it was two stories high.

"It's really solid," Ken said proudly. "Those walls are made of top-quality fir four-by-sixes laid on top of each other in courses and spiked together! To make the openings for windows, I built the wall solid to where the top of the window would be, then carefully cut out the opening with a chain saw. I'm going to leave the wood plain on the inside, and cover the outside with cedar shingles.

"This house ought to last for a while!"

When I visited Ken again that summer, his house was nearly finished. The soft grain of the wood glowed in the light of a kerosene lamp. An Oriental rug and a fleecy sheepskin lay on the polished hemlock floor. California redwood framed the windows. Not much remained to be done. "But right now I have to concentrate on setting up my workshop," he said. "I have several orders backed up for instruments. It's time to go back to work."

For me, it was time to go east and south. Meredith and I began by driving the North Cascades Highway, which winds through some of the most breathtaking mountain scenery in the world. Once across the Cascade Range, we turned south for Yakima, where we joined Lynn Buchanan and Judy Beehler. Lynn is a businessman and Air Force reserve officer; Judy teaches in an elementary school. Both are pilots, members of the ski patrol, and officers of mountain rescue organizations. That afternoon the four of us set off on a trail that climbs into the heart of the Goat Rocks Wilderness south of Mount Rainier National Park.

Lynn led the way, setting a slow, steady pace that covered the uphill miles without leaving the rest of us puffing and panting. He encouraged us by remarking that the next day's trail would be "all downhill."

It *was* downhill—for a while. But before long it headed up to crest a ridge. As we climbed a series of switchbacks, Meredith called out: "I thought you said today's trail would be all downhill."

"But it is," Lynn replied instantly. "We're just going the other way on it!"

It was the last week in July, and the temperature in Yakima had been hovering near 100°F. Here, at an elevation of 6,000 feet, spring flowers bloomed in the cool, crisp air. We hiked through meadows spangled with yellow buttercups and cinquefoils. We paused for a close look at a mariposa lily, whose three white petals, covered on the inner surfaces with soft hairs, have given it the common name of cat's ear.

We wound along the ridge, then descended to a steep cirque and Goat Lake, still covered with ice. To the east thrust the Goat Rocks—graphic evidence of the ancient glaciers that relentlessly carved volcanic rock into pinnacles.

The next morning we walked north for a couple of miles along the Pacific Crest Trail, the famed 2,400-mile scenic hiking route that reaches from the Mexican to the Canadian border. Just above Packwood Glacier we turned eastward and began climbing a peak called Old Snowy. Within an hour we had reached the 7,930-foot summit, and I signed my name in a summit register—the first time I had done so. I count Old Snowy the first "real" mountain I ever climbed. The thrill of that achievement almost outweighed the marvelous view from the top, with Mounts Rainier, Adams, and St. Helens— destined to erupt eight months later—all clearly visible.

After we returned to Yakima, Judy and I continued to Leavenworth, Washington. From a point a few miles outside this picturesque little town, which prides itself on its Bavarian atmosphere, we hiked to Colchuck Lake. Skirting its bright blue waters, we climbed another 2,100 feet up Aasgard Pass to the Enchantment Lakes.

Next day we set out to explore the surrounding plateau. Boulders lay strewn about; alpine wild flowers hugged the ground; a chain of tiny lakes reflected the sky and the ridges rimming the valley. Late snow persisted in shaded nooks, and a miniature iceberg drifted in a tarn at the edge of a snowfield. After three days of wandering among the Upper and Lower Enchantment Lakes, I could understand why Judy had chosen the spot as her favorite place in all the world.

To the south, one of my own favorite places was awaiting my summertime visit: Crater Lake National Park. Before my first visit the previous April, I had telephoned park headquarters from Portland, Oregon, to ask about the weather. Outside my hotel window a cheerful spring sun shone on flowers blooming in the city's parks.

"Is there snow at Crater Lake?" I asked.

"A lot of it has melted," came the reply, "but there's still about nine feet on the ground."

The road to Rim Village—the only one open then— wound between walls of snow. Across from the parking lot at the visitor center, a corrugated steel tunnel breached the snowbank; and from a window in its end I first saw the blue vision that is Crater Lake.

When I returned in August, the park bustled with activity. Crowds lined the overlook at Rim Village. I joined a group gathered around a model of the park. A ranger explained to us how Crater Lake developed when an ancient volcano, Mount Mazama, erupted and then collapsed inward 6,600 years ago. Much later another, smaller eruption inside the caldera built up the cone called Wizard Island.

*Loggers reap a rich harvest of timber from the western slopes of the Cascades. Below, the giant steel claw of a loader drops toward logs cut from a mountainside overlooking Black Oak Creek in the Mount Baker National Forest near Darrington, Washington. The loader will stack the timber on trucks for transport to the mill. Opposite, the rigging crew wraps steel chokers around logs so the main-line cable can drag them to the loader. Foreman Joe Prince (center), known as a hook tender, helps his brother, Wayne (right), a rigging slinger, and choker setter Doug Faddis. Harry Martin (at far right), owner of the logging firm, calls his foreman "the best hook tender I ever saw in 33 years of logging."*

*Most frequently climbed snowcapped mountain in the Western Hemisphere, Mount Hood seems to slumber peacefully on a soft bed of clouds. Each year thousands of hikers reach its 11,235-foot summit—highest point in Oregon. Although more than a century has passed since its last minor eruption, steam and gas vents still bear witness to the intense heat deep beneath the mountain.*

Water from rain and melting snow gradually accumulated in the great crater, which has no outlet. Today the lake collects about as much water as it loses through evaporation and seepage, and its level remains remarkably constant. At 1,932 feet, Crater Lake is the deepest in the United States.

My Cascade summer came to a close with a visit to Lassen Peak in northern California. Two residents of the area, Ralph and Virginia Lockyear, offered to show me the vicinity of Lassen Volcanic National Park. Outside the northwest entrance, Ralph pointed to a large boulder field.

"That area was once a good hay field," he told me. "Then on May 19, 1915, after nearly a year of eruptions, a river of mud and rock flowed down the mountainside. When it subsided, it left so many rocks that the land hasn't been used for anything except grazing to this day."

Three days after the mudflow, Lassen erupted again, this time explosively. A great avalanche of superheated steam, gases, and fragments of lava blasted outward along the route of the mudflow, uprooting and snapping off trees as far as three miles away.

I hiked the well-maintained trail to the 10,457-foot summit. From there I could look down the entire path of the mudflow, still officially termed the Devastated Area.

Another day my guide was retired Chief Ranger Lester D. Bodine. We hiked down the trail to Bumpass Hell, a thermal area named in the 1860s for its unfortunate discoverer, Kendall V. Bumpass; his leg was scalded when he stepped into a thermal pool. Around us clouds of steam roared from openings in the ground, and the rotten-egg smell of hydrogen sulfide hung in the air. Bubbles of steam in boiling mudpots rose to the surface and broke with a steady plop-plop.

"Water seeps through the earth," Lester explained, "and is heated by a large pool of molten rock far underground. The steam then returns to the surface, escaping through vents called fumaroles, or through hot springs or mudpots. All this heat shows there's still a lot of activity down there, and Lassen Peak could erupt again someday. Its last major eruption was in 1917, and it sputtered in 1921. In geological terms, that's less than an instant ago."

As we were leaving the park, Lester pointed out a ridge off to the south. "There runs Deer Creek Canyon," he said. "Somewhere beyond it, the volcanic Cascades end and the granitic Sierra Nevada begins."

My visit to the Cascades, too, had reached its end. I looked once more at Lassen Peak, and I recalled a poem written by one of Judy Beehler's sixth-grade students:

*Mountains stand alone*
*above the rest of the world . . .*
*just sky is higher.*

# Canada's Coast Mountains

*Steaming along a steep mountainside, the* Royal Hudson *skirts placid Horseshoe Bay, British*

*By* RALPH GRAY
*Photographed by* DAVID FALCONER

*Columbia, en route from North Vancouver to Squamish at the north end of Howe Sound.*

RALPH GRAY, NATIONAL GEOGRAPHIC STAFF

*Tumbling northwestward from the Fraser River, the Coast Mountains fringe the Pacific into fjords that reach inland to the base of glacier-clad peaks. A single paved road and two rail lines traverse the formidable barrier to reach British Columbia's interior. Geologists describe the Coast Mountains as a mass of granitic and metamorphic rock uplifted relatively recently—about ten million years ago.*

As CANADA'S VOYAGEURS pushed westward to explore that vast land, they overcame one geographic obstacle after another: the dense eastern forests, the granite hills and twining lakes of the Canadian Shield, the endless plains, the Rocky Mountains.

At last the early Canadians were free, surely, to step to the Pacific Ocean and complete their continental conquest. But no; still another barrier stood in the way. A jumbled, almost pathless mountain system complicated by icefields and fierce canyons rose before them, forming a barricade more than 950 miles long and 35 to 100 miles wide.

These were the Coast Mountains, so forbidding that when Simon Fraser in 1808 found a way around them by descending the river named for him, everyone followed suit—or found another detour. Thus began a pattern of bypassing the Coast Mountains, and its results are still etched on the map of British Columbia, the huge province that contains almost the entire reach of the range.

Fully half of all British Columbians live in Vancouver and the "lower mainland" near the mouth of the Fraser. From many parts of the city you can look across the harbor and see the southern ramparts of the Coast Mountains. Suburbs have taken root on the lowest slopes, but above them an unbroken mantle of Douglas fir rises sharply to jagged outcrops spangled with snowbanks even in midsummer.

While in Vancouver I took an informal poll of people I met. "What do you call those mountains that begin across the harbor?" I asked.

"You mean Grouse Mountain?"

"I call them the 'north shore mountains.' "

"Just 'the mountains,' I guess."

I offered a hint: "Where are the Coast Mountains?"

"I don't know about them."

"Aren't they farther up the coast?"

Hardly anyone I encountered had heard of Mount Waddington, the highest mountain wholly within British Columbia, jutting 13,177 feet skyward only 175 air miles northwest of Vancouver. It was as though the "north shore mountains" had been put there merely as a scenic backdrop for the city; what lay beyond was as remote and unknown as Tibet.

My intent was to breach this empty realm of rock and ice as best I could by car, boat, aircraft, and oversnow tracked vehicle. My companions would be my wife, Jean, and photographer David Falconer, both Canadian born, both veteran travelers in their native land. On a glorious July day, we drove to Horseshoe Bay at the end of the mainland portion of the Trans-Canada Highway.

From here, as we headed northward, Provincial Route 99 passed along a narrow ledge between Howe Sound on the west and a mountain wall on the east. At the head of the sound sat Squamish in a pall of sulfur fumes from the pulp mill south of town. People here are grateful for the brisk north wind they call a "squamish."

"When you reach Squamish, you're just about at the end of things," an elegant Vancouver lady had told us on the flight from the East Coast. But for us, this was the beginning. In a couple of miles the air had cleared and we were staring upward almost in disbelief at Mount Garibaldi and the peaks and glaciers beyond. So must Capt. George Henry Richards have reacted when, in 1860, standing on the deck of his survey ship in Howe Sound, he beheld a majestic peak soaring 8,787 feet above sea level. He named it for the Italian patriot Giuseppe Garibaldi.

Today Garibaldi Provincial Park preserves a choice section of the Coast Mountains. Side roads from the highway offer access but stop short of the boundary. Inside is an unspoiled retreat for cross-country skiers in winter, backpackers in summer. But summer had arrived late, and the access roads were empty. Throughout those first days Jean, David, and I were constantly struck by the apparent lack of recreational use of the mountains. Although vans and campers, each topped by the mandatory canoe, rolled along the highway, seldom did we see a vehicle at a campsite, and never a canoe on a lake or river. Later we would learn how untypical this was. But for the moment, the mountains belonged to us alone, especially after we left the Pemberton Valley area of lush farms. We took a gravel "summer only" road of switchbacks and precipices that is not even shown on most maps. Driving carefully, we crawled in a cloud of our own dust past Duffey Lake and Indian reserves to the town of Lillooet, completing our first traverse of the Coast Mountains.

To reach the next traverse we had to drive far inland along British Columbia's "main street"—Provincial Route 97—which leads from Vancouver northward up the Fraser River Valley to Prince George and on to Dawson Creek. At Williams Lake we turned west on a paved road that soon changed to gravel. For hours we churned along, occasionally passing a ranch-country town or an Indian community. Picnicking beside the southeast-flowing Chilcotin River, we got our first signal of the invisible mountains somewhere to the west. The waters of the river were the unmistakable milky-blue hue that says "glacial melt."

Soon, like a mirage across the dusty land, the glacier-ridden ranges appeared, growing larger, higher, and more three-dimensional with every mile of our approach.

This was all pleasantly familiar to Jean and me. Twenty-six years before, we had thrilled at our first glimpses of these mountains as we followed the track of explorer Alexander

Mackenzie for a NATIONAL GEOGRAPHIC article. At that time the road ended at Anahim Lake. Only with the help of half a dozen key people were we able to continue by jeep and horseback to the Bella Coola Valley, where Mackenzie reached Pacific waters in 1793 after his long journey from Montreal. Now Jean and I wondered whether any of our friends of long ago would still be in the area.

DESCENDING into the narrow valley is still a memorable experience. The "citizen's road," surveyed and bulldozed by dedicated but amateur Bella Coola residents, narrows to one lane and drops 4,000 feet in 12 miles. Fortunately we met no upcoming traffic. Arriving safely on the valley floor, we headed for the airstrip, where Dave Kahl of Wilderness Airlines was expecting us. The weather and light were perfect for a flight over Waddington, 90 miles to the southeast. With David Falconer and me aboard, Dave skillfully circled his Cessna 185 up and out of the valley.

"You fellows are lucky," he shouted above the engine's roar. "Usually this wild stretch is hidden by clouds or storms." Below us, the world was all glaciers, snowfields, and serrated ridges, with an occasional dark peak jutting starkly through the dazzling whiteness. Soon we were circling Mount Waddington, which rose in regal grandeur, confident in its domination of an entire province. A light crown of clouds rested serenely on its triple summits.

I marveled at our easy "conquest." Back in Vancouver, when asking people about Waddington, I had met one person who knew all about it. Phyllis Munday reached the northwest summit in 1928 with her late husband, Don, and his brother, Bert—the first party to climb on Waddington.

"Some people wanted to name it Mount Munday," Mrs. Munday told Jean and me in the living room of her North Vancouver home. "But my husband thought it should be named for the railroad promoter Alfred Waddington."

"But there's a painting labeled 'Mount Munday,' " Jean said, pointing to one of a dozen photographs and paintings of mountains on the walls.

"That's a slightly smaller peak near Waddington," Mrs. Munday said. "It is named for us. We were the first to climb it—in 1930—as well as nearby Jubilee Mountain, in 1931.

"I'm glad we went in those days," she continued. "We had to devise all our own clothing and equipment and find our own way. We usually came in by way of Knight Inlet. Then we had to bushwhack up the Franklin River and climb Franklin Glacier to get to the base of the mountains.

"Today most climbers come in from the interior, flying to a lake or glacier near the peak. Lots of people see mountains as just something to climb and then go home. They

have sold their wilderness souls to the flying machine."

I recalled those words now as I looked down, admittedly without too much guilt, at the frigid terrain sliding smoothly under our plane on the flight back to Bella Coola.

Waiting at the landing strip when we returned at 9 p.m. was Dennis Gaarden, now a prospering businessman, whom we had known as a 12-year-old on our previous visit. The restaurants in the valley were closed, so it seemed natural to be taken to Dennis's mother's house for dinner. In 1953, when there were no public eating or sleeping places in the valley, we had roomed and boarded with the Gaardens.

After greetings all around, we caught up on the changes of a quarter century. Gudrun Gaarden's husband, Jalmer, had died and now she was married to Haakon Brekke, who had been Jalmer's best man. The farmhouse had burned; it was replaced by a more compact home. But Gudrun's cooking was as tasty and her nature as generous as ever.

Gudrun is a living historical monument in Bella Coola. She was brought from Norway to the valley as an infant in 1913, and was adopted by a pioneering Norwegian couple, Helga and Bernard Jacobsen, who had settled here in 1894.

"We have the best of both (Continued on page 75)

*Swooping down from Grouse Mountain, Burke Ewing III and Veronique Marot guide their tandem hang glider toward a landing far below. Located just across the harbor from Vancouver, Canada's third largest city, the 3,974-foot mountain attracts hikers and skiers in season and provides a dramatic setting for hang-gliding demonstrations and an annual international meet.*

*Homeward bound, members of the Woodfibre pulp mill's day shift charge off the ferryboat* Garibaldi II. *The ferry crosses Howe Sound to link the isolated mill site with the rest of British Columbia's "lower mainland." The forest-products industry remains the province's mainstay. At right, a soaring stand of mixed conifers typifies B.C.'s 134 million acres of forest lands. The trees grow right down to water level at Princess Louisa Inlet, an arm of the fifty-mile-long Jervis Inlet.*

*Where Sasquatch, alias Bigfoot, may once have roamed, campers Coleen Fraser and Jim Newkirk await an aerial pickup. They stand at an elevation of 4,500 feet beside Ape Lake, a mountain gem flecked with tiny icebergs breaking off Fyles Glacier in the July sun. The lake's name supposedly comes from a sighting nearby of the legendary man-ape Sasquatch, possibly on Ape Glacier (right), the tongue of ice below pyramidal Mount Jacobsen and its slightly lower west peak. Opposite, a Wilderness Airlines pilot lands his DeHavilland Beaver to return the campers to Bella Coola, by air only 20 minutes away.*

worlds," said Dennis. "Sure, we're still isolated, in spite of the road. And the coastal ships don't stop anymore. But there's air service to take us outside when we want to go."

Jean and I went to the dock and found a robust man in his late 60s getting ready to go out in his gill-netter. It was Clayton Mack, the Bella Coola Indian fisherman who took us to Mackenzie Rock in 1953. "Yes, I remember," he said. "That boat blew up later on. An engine leak. Threw me right into the water. Some fellows came along and saved me."

Clayton and his two boats are often in demand by visitors who want to test new fishing waters, or perhaps just listen to the spellbinding Indian's tales—including those about "sightings" of Sasquatch, or Bigfoot, the elusive, apelike creature of West Coast folklore.

Before leaving Bella Coola Valley, we took to the air again on a short flight to Ape Lake, 4,500 feet above sea level. Our floatplane landed among small icebergs on an eye-drop of clear blue surrounded by enormous dark crags and crunching glaciers. Pilot Wayne Sissons was ferrying a couple for an outing in the wilderness.

"There are dozens of small lakes folks can have all to themselves," Wayne said. "It's the coming way to vacation. We fly 'em in, and later come back and get them."

TWEEDSMUIR PROVINCIAL PARK, British Columbia's largest, lay athwart our route in and out of Bella Coola Valley. It encompasses 2,424,400 acres on the eastern slopes of the Coast Mountains. The preserve was named for the 15th Governor-General of Canada, John Buchan, Baron Tweedsmuir of Elsfield.

The titled Scot, equally well known as novelist *(The Thirty-nine Steps)* and statesman when he came to Canada in 1935, turned his largely ceremonial assignment into a serious tour of duty. In 1937 he traveled extensively in this region, which had not changed much since that other notable Scot, Alexander Mackenzie, had passed through 144 years earlier. Lord Tweedsmuir wrote: "I have now travelled over most of Canada and have seen many wonderful things, but I have seen nothing more beautiful and more wonderful than the great park which British Columbia has done me the honour to call by my name."

And still the park area has changed little since Mackenzie's time, especially in the south. At the northern reaches of Tweedsmuir, however, big industry has left its imprint. Kenney Dam blocks the Nechako River, creating the Nechako Reservoir and backing its waters up to the park boundary. The man-made lake is the main access to the northern part of the park, but an official pamphlet warns boaters of "drowned forests and floating debris."

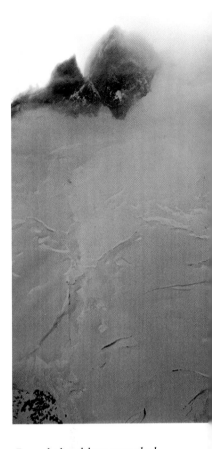

*Broad shoulders mantled with gleaming glaciers, Mount Waddington hides its head in a cloudcap. The highest mountain wholly within British Columbia remained little known until 1925. Then Phyllis Munday spotted it in her binoculars; and three years later she, her husband, and her brother-in-law climbed to the northwest summit. William House and Fritz Wiessner scaled the central peak (above)—the true summit—in 1936.*

*Midsummer album: Accompanied by her stuffed dog, "called Bear to keep away real bears," Bonnie Carey takes to the trail in Tweedsmuir Provincial Park. The hike was a break in the park's work-training program for British Columbia teen-agers. Late-afternoon sun backlights cypress foliage in the Bella Coola Valley; saxifrage borders a rivulet near Duffey Lake; and a young porcupine bristles in fright. Opposite, a cyclist takes a dip in a beaver pond beside the highway near Terrace.*

The reservoir is part of Alcan's aluminum-making complex centered at Kitimat. The water rises almost to the crest of the Coast Mountains; then a ten-mile tunnel drops it to just above sea level at Kemano. A large generating plant converts the force of the plunging water to electricity and transmits it by a 51-mile power line to Kitimat. There an electrolytic smelter sits beside a deepwater port where freighters from Australia and elsewhere unload bauxite concentrate.

Before visiting Kitimat we had some other interesting geography to cover. We ate dust on the road back to Williams Lake, turned north on a seeming treadmill to Prince George, then inched west again into the mountains along the Yellowhead Highway. This fine road follows a natural river-system pathway through the Coast Mountains. Without a single hard climb, it carries truckers and travelers clear to the Pacific at Prince Rupert.

Our journey took us past glacier-hung Hudson Bay Mountain to the falls at Moricetown on the Bulkley River, where we stopped to watch Carrier Indians gaffing salmon. Using poles 20 feet long, the fishermen probed the boiling waters for unseen fish poised to leap the falls in their determined pilgrimage upstream to the spot where they were hatched—there to spawn and die.

From Hazelton with its nearby "totem pole" Indian villages, we drove along the base of ice-crested Seven Sisters Peaks to the new, bustling northland town of Terrace. "Up here, a town of 10,000 seems like a metropolis," said the lady at our motel desk. Indeed it did. Lumberyards were stacked high along the Canadian National Railway tracks. Trucks careened through on their way to Prince Rupert or Kitimat. Canadian Pacific Air ran daily flights to Vancouver. The new Skeena Mall housed a complete shopping center.

We made Terrace the base for our side trips to Kitimat, the town established in 1953 to house Alcan's smelter workers; Prince Rupert, the growing port city with civic pride and an unlimited future; and Atlin, 400 miles northwest, where the Coast Mountains approach Yukon Territory. Roads lead to Atlin in a roundabout fashion, trending far away to the interior plains. The easiest way to see this untrammeled northern half of the mountains is by air. So we got in touch with Max Neubacher, bush pilot par excellence, who learned his aviation with the Luftwaffe early in World War II.

I felt safer in the air with Max than walking or driving on the streets of Terrace. He knew the tangled terrain intimately, and picked out a route of valleys and passes just east of the highest crests. Soon we were at the level of the snows, looking into an almost continuous reach of mountains and glaciers that mark the boundary between northern British Columbia and the Alaska Panhandle.

For three days this frozen, forbidding world would be my home. Leaving Jean beside the lake in the town of Atlin, David and I helicoptered south thirty turbulent miles toward the Boundary Ranges of the Coast Mountains en route to Camp 18 of the Juneau Icefield Research Program.

Almost immediately the blue waters and green forests ended, and the world of ice and rock began. Then, with nothing but white below us, suddenly there was nothing but white anywhere. The fog so prevalent on the Alaska side of the mountains had shifted across the crest ridges. The pilot made a quick U-turn out of the whiteout zone and landed us in bright sunlight at Camp 26 on the edge of massive Llewellyn Glacier.

Next morning we tried again. The copter returned and flew us farther south, up over Llewellyn's broad back until we saw a welcome speck on the snow below. As we descended, the speck turned into the bright orange Thiokol tracked vehicle that was to take us another ten miles to Camp 18.

WITH GARY LINDER at the vehicle's controls, we crossed the divide into Alaska. We were now on the Matthes Glacier, on a sparkling day. Before us lay a vast expanse of ice; far across it we could see the jagged ramparts of the icefield's peripheral peaks sixty miles to the south.

At Camp 18, a main highland field headquarters for the icefield research program, Dr. Maynard M. Miller strode out to meet us. We had known each other for years, and it was good to see him here on his "home ground."

"Yes, this is my 34th summer in the icefields, and rarely have I seen a better day," Maynard said over coffee. "You know, we probably have some of the worst weather in the world. It comes from the Pacific. Thirty-four miles south of here, Lemon Creek Glacier gets 150 inches of precipitation a year; across the divide, Atlin has 11 inches. That explains all the glacial buildup here in the Boundary Ranges.

"When we first started coming here in the 1940s, we spent about 90 percent of our time surviving and 10 percent in research. Now those figures are reversed. In an area of about 5,000 square miles we have 15 main stations and 20 lesser camps, with about 60 people—students and staff."

Through the years, Maynard and his associates have amassed a body of information about their glacial and mountain environment unequaled anyplace else. Scientists around the world are interested in short-term climatic changes, as well as the dramatic question of whether there's going to be another ice age. Experts agree that studying glaciers over a long period is one of the best ways to pursue the answers.

The sun was bright enough the next day to hold morning classes for some of the students on a shelf of rock overlooking Gilkey Glacier and the Vaughan Lewis Icefall. But by

*Rugged men in a rugged country: Clayton Mack, aboard his gill-netter at the Bella Coola wharf, prepares to cast off for his almost daily bout with chancy waters and elusive salmon. A Bella Coola Indian in his late 60s, Mack fishes a network of inlets and channels reaching a hundred miles to the open Pacific. Opposite, Wayne Ridgway, a master with a chain saw, shapes huge spruce trees to create "British Columbia's largest log building"—to serve as his home and a pub on the highway between Terrace and Kitimat.*

*Using 20-foot poles, Carrier Indians gaff salmon fighting their way upstream over falls of the Bulkley River. The Bulkley joins the Skeena River at Hazelton; together they provide the only easily traveled natural passage through the Coast Mountains. The Skeena reaches Hecate Strait near the busy Pacific port of Prince Rupert. Opposite, Chuck Long grades fish—mostly king and sockeye salmon—at the Prince Rupert Fishermen's Cooperative Federation. As huge catches from the sea move past him, he separates them by type, size, and quality.*

noon, wisps of fog were moving insidiously up Gilkey Trench from the sea. When we left Camp 18 at 2 p.m., the whiteout had returned, and we could see only about 30 feet. Soon the whiteout was total, and I felt like a weevil inside an enormous boll of cotton.

Somehow Gary Linder, craning out the side and following a previous track, found "the junction"—marked by three large fuel drums—where five snow trails intersected, and where we must turn north to find our way back to British Columbia. For two more hours we crawled upward and across the broad divide. And then the vehicle was laboring less, and our speed increased. We had passed the invisible international boundary at the glacier crest and were going downgrade. Slowly the whiteout thinned, and suddenly the sun was back in the sky and we were in the real world.

FROM THE AIR, Atlin looks lonely and lost between vast reaches of sparse sprucelands to the east and the "great water" that inspired its name. And it *is* almost lost to the rest of British Columbia. Atlin Lake forms a southern source of the Yukon River. Thus geography causes the town's several hundred residents to look not south to Vancouver but north to Whitehorse, the capital of Yukon Territory, as their trade and travel center.

I had written to an Atlin family—United States expatriates who had reported on their life in a wilderness cabin for the National Geographic *School Bulletin*. Bruce and Jeaneil Johnson and their daughter, Zea, came skimming across the lake in a 21-foot Teslin Indian canoe to take us to their home on the Atlin River. What struck me first about the place was not that it was in the wilderness, but that it was indeed a home. A large, comfortably furnished living room merged into a kitchen that looked out across an amazingly productive garden. "The garden is mine," said Jeaneil. "And I milk the nanny goat," said 7-year-old Zea, blue eyes dancing. "We have 2 goats, 25 chickens, 45 dogs, and 2 cats."

"I guess I'll take credit for the dogs," said her father. His charges were staked out in clearings on both sides of the house. Bruce is developing his own strain of Alaskan husky, a mix with Labrador and some Siberian blood. In summer he trains the dogs by hitching them to an old Volkswagen.

"Breeding, feeding, and training are the keys to sled-dog racing," said Bruce, who has won both 70-mile and 160-mile races at Atlin. In March 1980, seven months after our visit, Bruce and his dogs finished a highly laudable 14th in the Iditarod, the 1,200-mile run from Anchorage to Nome.

"Bruce hunts game for most of our meat," said Jeaneil. "He guides wilderness parties. I sell occasional articles to magazines. We've never been hungry, even though we're truly isolated in November and December when the lake is freezing, in May and June when it's thawing, and often in September and October when big winds sweep across. But we'd rather be here than in a city."

Here our Coast Mountains odyssey ended. On the long flight back to Terrace and the longer drive to Vancouver, we reflected on all we had seen and learned. We had looked at much harsh terrain, but we had also sought out the quiet places and their sturdy inhabitants—and seen that not everyone, after all, had followed Simon Fraser's example and avoided these magnificent mountains.

Our final weekend in Canada was a three-day holiday in August. This time, in contrast to quiet July, we found outdoor vacationers everywhere—at Alice Lake and Golden Ears Provincial Parks, and of course on Grouse Mountain with its popular skyride. But the biggest eye-opener came when we returned to Garibaldi Provincial Park. At the Black Tusk Nature Conservancy Area, both parking lots were overflowing. Latecomers—young couples from Vancouver, mostly—were finding spots for their cars along the road wherever they could, shouldering backpacks, and disappearing into the depths of the park.

Now we knew that—like the Alps and the Rockies in their time—the Coast Mountains are also changing from a barrier to a goal.

*At spectacular Gilkey Trench in the Boundary Ranges, David Vost of the University of New Brunswick and Michael Bruzga of Dartmouth College survey glacier movement. Meanwhile the special instrument at far right records the duration of sunshine each day. Maynard M. Miller directs these and other studies of the Juneau Icefield Research Program. At right, Dr. Miller lectures to a group of students overlooking some of "the most magnificent field laboratory views on earth."*

FOLLOWING PAGES:
*Craggy peaks called
nunataks create
shadow plays on the
pure white screen of
the Taku Glacier in the
Alaska Panhandle,
just west of the
British Columbia
boundary. The northern
reaches of the Coast
Mountains present
frozen grandeur on
an almost limitless scale.*

In their outboard-propelled freight canoe, Jeaneil, Zea, and Bruce Johnson cross Tagish Lake to their wilderness homestead on the Atlin River. The good earth provides them with firewood, garden vegetables, game, and fish. For cash income, Bruce raises and races sled dogs, whose summer training includes pulling a stripped Volkswagen along an abandoned railroad right-of-way.

FOLLOWING PAGES: Warm summer sun and mountains that never shed winter look down on anglers casting for arctic grayling in Atlin Lake, a source of the north-flowing Yukon River.

# Mount McKinley

*By* SALLIE M. GREENWOOD
*Photographed by* GALEN ROWELL

*this sloping platform at 16,200 feet before continuing their ascent of the Alaska giant.*

"IT'S SO VERY MUCH higher than you're used to looking," mused Roger Moseley. "It's so *massive*. It's awesome." My three tentmates and I were lazing away a hot afternoon in late May on the Kahiltna Glacier, staying out of the intense, reflected glare of the sun and waiting for evening's coolness before carrying supplies farther up North America's highest mountain.

Mount McKinley, 135 miles north of Anchorage, shoulders its way above other peaks of the Alaska Range to an isolated, magnificent elevation of 20,320 feet. Fifteen of us had taken up the challenge to traverse McKinley—ascending one side, descending another—a challenge indifferently thrown down by a mountain whose snows are permanent and whose weather is capricious and often severe.

Thirteen days later and 11,100 feet higher, leader Jim Hale remarked, "I've got to admit that this is one of the most complete climbing experiences I've ever led. You guys have seen everything."

"Great," I thought, scrunching deeper into the warmth of my down parka, "and we haven't reached the top yet."

We were at 18,200-foot Denali Pass, a black-rock and white-snow gash between McKinley's South Peak—the summit—and the 19,470-foot North Peak. Seven of our group had squeezed into the relative warmth of a thin nylon tent to talk about food, weather, events of the climb, our impressions poetic and mundane. Voices competed with the roar of the small, pressurized gasoline stove as we melted snow in a precariously balanced, carefully tended stainless-steel pot.

Jim's "everything" included the best and the worst that McKinley has to offer climbers—and even the unique.

The best: sunny, still days; time uncluttered by schedules; the almost overwhelming superscale of mountains and sky that seemed to reduce us to lilliputian size; the joy of running downhill on snowshoes through untracked powder tinged orange by the setting sun; hours of happy concentration as we climbed the snow and ice of the 40°-angled West Buttress; the solid satisfaction of leading my roped partners up a steep ridge of rock and wind-packed snow to cache food for our next camp at 17,200 feet.

The worst: deaths of two Korean men—one an Everest veteran—in a 1,500-foot fall; time-consuming, energy-draining rescue and evacuation of four other climbers who were either sick or injured, including one of our own party; an unheard-of breach of mountain ethics, a theft from a cache of our food and equipment; crevasses; loss of supplies to raiding ravens; heavy winds and subzero temperatures.

And the unique: encountering two dog teams that had been on the mountain more than a month. One had mushed all the way to the summit—a first in the mountain's history.

Right now, as we talked in the tent, McKinley was giving us a sample of its worst weather: strong winds, blowing snow, and bitter cold. "Any time you walk outside and get blown off your feet," Jim told us, "I reckon that to be at least 70 miles an hour."

We had just spent most of a bone-chilling morning putting up three tents that had blown down between 1 and 3 a.m. We had mended broken aluminum tent poles with tape and ski-pole splints, and laboriously sawed blocks of snow to build walls around the tents, incorporating packs, snowshoes, and plastic sleds—anything to deflect the wind that slammed through the pass.

"I don't have a sense of impending doom," I had softly assured my tape recorder after our tent went down—whispering so as not to disturb Roger or Hank Bahnson, both of whom dozed through the storm. Just above my face the tent billowed, flapped, and shuddered; fine snow, driven through the closed zippers of door and windows, dusted my sleeping bag. "I'm warm. The tent's collapsed but it's intact. We have food and fuel. We're O.K. Don't panic."

Two months before, I had talked with Barbara Washburn, first woman to climb McKinley and, after 33 years, still one of only two women to have climbed both the South and North Peaks (college instructor Joanna Coleman became the other in 1974). We met on a rainy day in Boston. Barbara reminisced briskly: "We wouldn't have attempted the summit if the weather hadn't been reasonably good. Getting caught in a storm on the South Peak would be a nightmare."

Her husband, Brad, told me that their party had waited out violent storms for more than a week at Denali Pass. When at last the weather improved, they climbed the two peaks on successive days.

"I'm particularly glad I did the North Peak," Barbara said, "because I don't have happy memories of the South Peak. There it was 20° below zero, cloudy, windy, and miserable. But the North Peak was marvelous. We had a breathtaking view. That's what makes it all worthwhile."

On the morning of the fourth day in Denali Pass, Jim Hale edged his large frame through the tent door. Tom Blair and I shifted farther toward our end of the tent while Hank—steadying the pot on the stove—and Roger shrugged toward their end. Sleeping bags, foam pads, down clothing, boots, a bag of food, and plastic cups, all in ordered confusion, nearly filled the tent. We cleared a space for Jim.

"It looks bad," he said. "I think we've got to assume that it's going to get worse."

We felt strong and—given good weather—perfectly capable of climbing the remaining 2,100 feet of elevation to the summit. But it didn't appear that the weather was going

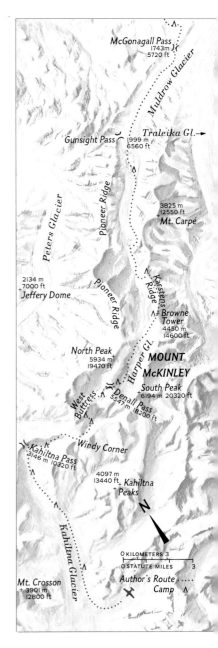

*Named McKinley in 1896, the twin-peaked mountain that natives called Denali, the Great One, became part of a national park in 1917. The author's traverse took 22 days.*

to break. We needed to decide: Should we keep waiting for a suitable day for the summit attempt, sacrificing the traverse?—for we wouldn't have enough food to do both. Or should we complete the traverse and forget about the summit?

I recalled a bit of McKinley's history: a day in June 1912. "The game's up; we've got to get down!" shouted artist-explorer Belmore Browne to one of his partners when he decided to turn back only yards from the summit. It would have been the first ascent; but he was finally defeated by the heavy winds. "The breath was driven from my body," he wrote, "and I held to my axe with stooped shoulders to stand against the gale; I couldn't go ahead."

Ours was a group decision: Reluctantly, we would settle for the traverse.

We had been on McKinley for 17 days. Now we knew that within a week's time flowing streams, green tundra, and wild flowers would replace the stark, sterile beauty of the snow and rock that surrounded us.

THE NAMED FEATURES of McKinley's northeast flank, the side we would descend, were as familiar to us as family history. We had read accounts of early expeditions, and pored over Bradford Washburn's shaded relief map and his crisp black-and-white photographs. The mountain had first been climbed from this side: Prospectors reached the top of the North Peak in 1910, and the true summit, the South Peak, was attained in 1913 by a party led by Hudson Stuck, Episcopal Archdeacon of the Yukon.

Wind pushed us down the marble-hard snow of the Harper Glacier, named for Alaskan Walter Harper, first to stand atop the South Peak. The only marks of our passing were the ten evenly spaced punctures made at each step by the spikes of our crampons.

"Where's the poetry now?" A rhetorical question posed by Roy Keenan blew past me on the wind as we waited for York Rentsch to right his heavily laden sled. Several hours later and 3,100 feet below Denali Pass, we camped where the white satin of the Harper's snow and ice crumples and cascades another 2,900 feet to the Muldrow Glacier, just even with the tawny granite buttress of Browne Tower.

The key to bypassing the Harper Icefall is Karstens Ridge, just below Browne Tower. The ridge is a steep ramp to the Muldrow, only inches wide in one section along its crest where it plummets dramatically 5,500 feet to the Traleika Glacier on one side and 2,000 feet to the Muldrow on the other.

Care. Concentration. Tom admitted to humming endless choruses of "Jesus Loves Me! This I Know" as he worked his way down; my own mantra was simply *Concentrate, concentrate,* broken by fragments of "Paper Roses."

I was mightily grateful to be going down rather than carrying loads up this narrow spine. Archdeacon Stuck named it for one of his companions, Harry Karstens, who had helped cut "a staircase three miles long in the shattered ice" of the earthquake-jumbled ridge on their ascent.

After Karstens Ridge we had but two more obvious hazards ahead: Ten miles of hiking on the heavily crevassed Muldrow Glacier, and crossing the roiling, braided streams of glacier-fed McKinley River.

WE HAD REHEARSED crevasse rescue in Anchorage, and had joked about crevasses for the last three weeks. We even counted the number of times our companions had punched through to snow-concealed cracks in the active glaciers. Fortunately no one had gone in entirely.

In 1913 Harry Karstens wrote in his diary: ". . . I started over crevas snow bridge gave way but I was pulld back. Could not see bottom. . . ."

I, too, investigated a crevasse on the Muldrow Glacier, as briefly as did Karstens. It was not hidden; it advertised itself wholly, and appeared to offer a solid snow bridge. Others had already crossed, leaving tracks deep in the snow. Tom and York moved across and braced for me; photographer Galen Rowell stood off to one side, his team of Roger and Hank watching with amused interest and awaiting their turn.

I shuffled ahead. Then, suddenly, I tripped over the tips of my snowshoes and fell asprawl. My right arm, thrown out to catch my weight, broke through the snow bridge. Snow chilled the side of my face as I stared into the depths, into shades of light blue, bottomless, incredibly clear, surreal.

As I pitched forward, Tom pulled the rope tight. I kicked and rolled, hampered by my pack, my camera strap, a ski pole. Galen shouted encouragement.

*Safe.*

There was the nervous laughter of relief. Sunshine. Warmth. We went on.

In another day we reached McGonagall Pass and 200 feet of scrambling up loose rock, gravel, and boulders wet with snowmelt. Gulls wheeled above. I was aware of small plants with purple flowers. I saw a spider.

We were off the mountain.

There remained a grueling two-day march across tundra, springy green carpet instead of endless snow. We forded the McKinley—crossing at 2:30 a.m., before daytime glacial melt made it more hazardous—and walked into a spruce forest, breathing in the welcoming smell of damp earth.

A last look back. McKinley is shrouded in gray clouds. There is no hint of the highest mountain in North America. But we know. We were there.

*Aided by a line fixed by an earlier party, York Rentsch (opposite) tops the West Buttress. Above, the author takes a fudge break before continuing the supply "carry" to the next camp; Hal Winton, his pack emptied, grins with relief.*

Of 533 climbers attempting Mount McKinley
in 1979, two died in a fall and ten needed
rescue or evacuation. Above, right,
mountaineers gently move West German
Andreas Kahnt toward a waiting helicopter;
at right, the copter carries the victim of
altitude-induced cerebral edema up and
away from Denali Pass. Above, Rolf Haas
of Switzerland, who has just broken his
ankle, stoically watches as physician Hank
Bahnson prepares an injection at Windy
Corner. By remarkable good fortune, Haas
reached an Anchorage hospital within eight
hours of his accident. Climbers sledded
him 3,500 feet down the Kahiltna Glacier,
radioed a passing ski plane, and
rendezvoused with it in clearing weather. The
author's party helped with these and two
other rescues, one involving a pulmonary-
edema victim from their own group.

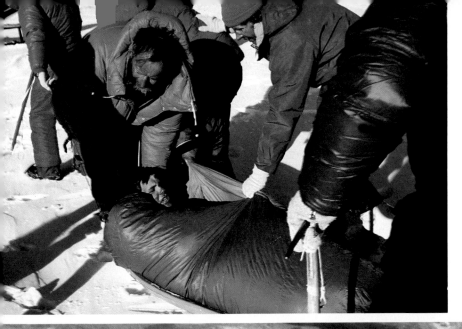

High winds, blowing snow, and bitter cold lock climbers at Denali Pass for three days. "The summit lost its significance in the face of this storm," reports the author. "Completing the traverse—and survival—had more appeal." Still dusted with snow, York Rentsch (below) musters energy to remove mittens and boots before returning to his sleeping bag.

FOLLOWING PAGES: *Step by cautious step, Vera Hollingshead edges around a cornice of snow while descending Karstens Ridge. Four days later the climbers forded the McKinley River to finish their traverse of Denali, the Great One.*

# Aspen's Rockies

*Early morning light tints North Maroon Peak and nearby ridges of the Elk Mountains. The*

*By* CYNTHIA RUSS RAMSAY
*Photographed by* ANNIE GRIFFITHS

*rugged beauty of the Colorado Rockies draws hundreds of thousands of visitors yearly.*

IN SUMMER, when the mountain meadows are lush with flowers and the furry marmots sun themselves on the heights, when waterfalls thunder into rivers swollen with snowmelt, Aspen becomes a town like no other on earth. A small community of homes and schools and churches, Aspen is also a center for activities so diverse it seems impossible they are all happening within a few miles of this one place.

Along Castle Creek, where the Aspen Music School holds its classes, New Yorker Nadia Ghent plays her violin—the strains of Brahms mingling with the melody of water rushing over rock.

In a forest still the haunt of elk and deer, college student Peter Didisheim starts up a series of steep switchbacks in the Maroon Bells-Snowmass Wilderness, and hikes to the windswept barrens above timberline.

On a verdant hillside glittering with iridescent blue damselflies, schoolteacher Jeannie Stonebrook of Memphis, Tennessee, practices a series of flowing movements of *T'ai chi ch'uan,* a highly disciplined Chinese form of exercise, at the Aspen Academy of Martial Arts in Snowmass Village.

Below the mottled pink cliffs of Browns Canyon, a white-topped wave crashes against the bow of a rubber raft, drenching Carol Murray of Tucson. The oarsman guiding the bucking, bouncing boat through Seidels Rapids ends the day's run down the Arkansas River in time for Carol to attend the ballet.

And as twilight shadows summits still gleaming with snow, the Gallagher family of Smoke Rise, New Jersey, watches rodeo-wise cowboys test their skills in bronc riding, calf roping, and steer wrestling.

On another evening I choose to stroll a brick-paved mall landscaped with petunia beds, graceful trees, and antique street lamps. The crowds—children with ice-cream cones, lean men in jeans and jogging shoes, smartly dressed, smiling women, a scattering of older couples in sweaters pulled on against the mountain chill—stop to listen to a string quartet performing out of doors. From time to time, someone drops a dollar into an open violin case.

Above the sweet melancholy of a Tchaikovsky andante, I can hear the shouts and cheers of spectators at a softball game in the park nearby.

Many of the sports shops, boutiques, bookstores, and galleries have not yet closed for the night; and here in this Colorado town almost 8,000 feet high, surrounded by the Rocky Mountain wilderness, I can buy Danish porcelain, Persian carpets, 19th-century English watercolors, cloisonné jewelry from China, as well as books and periodicals of remarkable variety, and equipment for virtually every athletic activity ever invented. Catering to the nearly 13,000 year-round residents of Pitkin County and the hundreds of thousands of vacationers each year from all over the world, the shops reflect opulent tastes and wide-ranging interests.

Yet in spite of its city sophistication and the Victorian charm of its gaily colored gabled and turreted houses, in spite of the seminars and concerts, discotheques and sidewalk cafés, it is the mountains that remain the fundamental fact of Aspen life.

Nestled in the valley of the Roaring Fork River between the Elk Mountains and the Sawatch Range, Aspen owes more than beauty and bracing climate to its highland setting, more than ski-season prosperity to the plunging slopes. The mountains bring more than the fragrance of spruce from their lofty forests; they offer more than a dramatic setting for golf courses, tennis courts, and Fourth of July fireworks. With their untrammeled snowfields and trailless woodlands, with their trout-filled streams and pristine lakes, with 20 peaks rising above 14,000 feet in Aspen's backyard, the mountains have a strong psychological impact on the town.

"I was never really sensitive to scenic beauty until I watched storms roll in across these peaks and moonlight turn their snowy crests to silver," said effervescent Houston socialite Kate Rivers.

"A new perspective comes out of living in the presence of these mountains. They dwarf everything else." She led me past a band playing bluegrass music to an outdoor buffet set up just below the 11,300-foot level of Aspen Mountain. With my plate piled high, I joined some 200 guests cheerfully celebrating summer on a lazy Sunday afternoon in July.

The mountains have taught Kevin Padden something else. Cross-country ski instructor in winter, kayaker in summer, Kevin looks for excitement in the backcountry all year long. "When I'm caught in a rapid on a river or challenged by a ski run, I'm so totally involved in the action that there's no time for the unimportant stuff—like flashy technique or style," he explained. "There's a special satisfaction that comes from doing something you put your whole self into."

For music student Tom Williams the mountains are an inspiration. For rancher Jon Hollinger they are a haven.

"I can escape the crowds by heading out on one of the trails," Jon said, tilting his hat—a "summer straw"—a little lower on his brow as our horses climbed the first steep rise. From the Hollinger ranch on Red Mountain, which faces the ski slopes across the Roaring Fork Valley, our destination was Bald Knob, a high grassy ridge that gave us a view of the Elk range from the green hulk of Mount Sopris to Italian Mountain. As we surrendered to the sweep of jagged peaks silhouetted sharply against an enamel sky, the wild grace of a soaring hawk, the timeless quiet of the forest, Aspen,

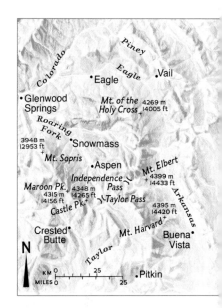

*Flanked by the Sawatch Range on the east and the Elk Mountains on the west, the former mining town of Aspen now reigns as Colorado's premier year-round resort. Offering four popular ski areas and a cultural feast of concerts, plays, and seminars, Aspen lies only minutes away from the wilderness of the southern Rocky Mountains.*

*Free as the wind, Paula Page and Jonathan Teuscher "ski the bumps" on Aspen Mountain. Another enthusiast, environmentalist Georgie Leighton (above), reminisces: "I've spent the last 15 winters skiing in Aspen—not well, but enjoying every minute!" Max Boté (top) teaches at Aspen Highlands Ski School, and at age 83 proclaims himself the oldest ski instructor in the world.*

somewhere in the valley far below, seemed nonexistent.

For people like Terry Young and Al Burnham, the mountains flanking the town offer snow almost the year around. Skiing was the magnet that lured them from Minnesota. Even when most of the high country has turned a glossy new green and diminutive flowers push up from the soil, Al, who designs skis, and Terry, who markets them, hike to reach the last great stretches of snow lingering in the north-facing bowls above tree line.

We were only 20 highway miles from Aspen when we shouldered our skis on a lustrous July morning and started up one of the white slopes rising above 12,095-foot Independence Pass on the Continental Divide. Our climb to the nearest high ridge was short, and the snow was soft enough that we could avoid sliding by kicking our boots in at each step. But I was still not acclimated to exertion at such elevations. In any case, with my weekend jogging and tennis and my occasional ski trips, I was no match for these ski mountaineers who regularly schuss headwalls and blast their way down avalanche chutes. I strained not to keep up but just to keep going, and thought wistfully of ski lifts. Yet even in the small effort of that short climb, I could sense what Terry means when he talks of "the world beyond sweat."

"It's a euphoria," Terry said, "that comes from pushing your own limits." It's the jubilation that gives the ski mountaineer's experience an extra glory. To Terry and Al and their friends, it's testing the edge of adventure, part of their Aspen way of life. To me it was a little glow of satisfaction that made the descent very sweet.

All too quickly, our skis carried us down. At snowline we paused to look at the impudent marsh marigolds blooming at our feet. For in the matchless landscape of the alpine tundra, wherever the snow melts, the earth surges with spring. Then we plodded back up into winter again, repeating the run until the snow began to get slushy in late morning.

Within minutes we were picnicking beside the tumbling waters of the Roaring Fork. Sipping snow-chilled white wine under a warm sun and a brilliant sky, with the mountains close above, we all agreed it was a superlative day.

Only a week later, when I set out to hike one of the many trails that start from the road below Independence Pass, the snow had retreated uphill and was honeycombed with bare patches. But other snowfields in the recesses of the Elk Mountains held out all summer.

I had begun that day at the Aspen Institute for Humanistic Studies, a brainchild of Chicago industrialist Walter P. Paepcke, whose wife, Elizabeth, discovered Aspen just before World War II. Overwhelmed by the splendor of its setting, Paepcke decided in 1945 to make Aspen a place as well

PRECEDING PAGES:
*Windswept peaks of
the Sawatch Range rise
above timberline to
elevations of more than
14,000 feet. About 65
to 70 million years ago,
enormous geologic forces
within the earth began to
cause massive uplifting of
an ancient inland seabed.
Much later, relentless
glaciers sculptured the
dramatic contours seen
today in this part of the
Colorado Rockies.*

known for its culture as for its scenery, where people could explore ideas as well as the great outdoors. Before his death in 1960, he had done so.

He launched the music festival that for 30 years has brought some of the world's finest musicians to perform here; and he organized the institute, whose schedule of public lectures and seminars on such matters as foreign policy, nuclear power, and genetics has helped make Aspen a mecca for people like Martin Fine, an attorney from Miami, Florida, and his wife, Pat.

"The institute gives the town an intellectual tradition other resorts just don't have," said Pat that morning on the way to a seminar on "The Shaping of the Arab World."

"If we simply wanted the outdoors, we could be in a hundred other places. But where else in the world could you meet such a variety of people! A cross section of all the interesting and all the interested people come here."

The institute is best known for its executive seminars—a program designed to immerse business and professional people in the humanities and broaden their outlook. In two-week sessions through much of the year, participants meet with leaders of government, labor, and the arts to discuss readings that range from Plato to T. S. Eliot.

I slipped into a session that was pondering what motivates people to work—a discussion prompted by a passage from the writings of Sigmund Freud. Stephen I. Schlossberg, director of the Washington, D. C., office of the United Auto Workers, was observing that "people work not just to have cars and country cabins. Self-esteem and standing in the community are important incentives. So is a pleasant social experience. We know that the happiest workers are the ones that have a chance to socialize on the job."

When the session adjourned for lunch and an afternoon raft trip on the Colorado River, 30 miles to the north, I joined my teen-age sons, David and Andrew, who had spent the morning playing golf. They were waiting for me at the Hotel Jerome, a renovated monument of the silver boom that lasted from 1879 to 1893. In those halcyon years, the silver barons built stately homes and many public buildings, including the Wheeler Opera House—now sheltering offices, a theater, and a boisterous pub—and the Jerome, once the pride of Aspen. The globe chandeliers, ornate fireplace, sweeping staircase, and gilt-edged mirror in the hotel's high-ceilinged lobby confirm that a taste for luxury has a long tradition in the town. The walk from the institute to the hotel took me through the quaint and quiet residential streets of the west end, where houses painted in cheerful colors and decorated with gingerbread trim, gables, and stained glass are redolent of the Victorian past.

The city council and civic groups have struggled hard to preserve the old charm of the town and the natural beauty of its surroundings. Zoning laws bar high-rise structures, billboards, and neon lights. Building codes determine structural details right down to types of windows.

Faced with a population that tripled between 1960 and 1975, Aspen adopted a controlled-growth policy that, along with the general inflation, has helped cause housing prices to streak skyward. A three-bedroom yellow cottage with blue trim that I admired would sell for at least $250,000.

The words of Sandy Glosser, who gave up an 18-room house in Dallas to live in a one-bedroom Aspen apartment with her daughter, help explain why people pay the astronomical prices: "You're not just buying living space. You're buying the mountains, the river, the snow, the ski slopes, and the stunning scenery."

A clear view of Aspen Mountain graced our table at the Hotel Jerome as I dined with my sons in the patio restaurant. I might have preferred to continue sitting there in the soft light, watching the small aspen leaves quake, watching them shimmer like spangles at every whisper of the wind; but I rallied at my sons' call for a hike, and we drove about 20 miles to the Linkins Lake trailhead.

The trail, well above timberline, took us across steeply rolling tundra, which in Colorado begins above 11,500 feet. Despite their morning of golf, the boys were soon far ahead of me. A little breathless, I caught up with them as they were skipping rocks on the jade-green waters of the lovely alpine lake, only half a mile around, lying at the base of a glacier-gouged ridge. It was a setting both intimate and grand.

The treeless expanse was broken only by boulders, the snow-webbed granite wall above the lake, and the jagged Sawatch crest off to the east. Dainty lavender daisies, yellow cinquefoils, and pink dwarf clovers brought me to my knees for a look at the miniature world of alpine flowers.

EVEN THAT wasn't close enough. "You have to lie flat to see half of the species," said Beatrice E. Willard a few days later. The robust, dynamic ecologist was sharing her knowledge and enthusiasm with a class on tundra sponsored by the Aspen Center for Environmental Studies.

"Small size is an advantage in the arctic climate of the tundra. Plants with small leaves, short stems, and few flowers more easily complete their growth in the brief, often interrupted summer. And growing close to the ground reduces exposure to wind and increases retention of solar heat," she told us as we jeeped to Taylor Pass in the Elk Mountains.

The narrow dirt road wound up through spruce and fir that gradually became more and more sparse, more and more

*On a dazzling March day, sisters Nina and Julie Bohlen glide through a wilderness world of sun and snow. Carried by tracked Sno-Cat nearly 2,000 feet up slopes of the Sawatch Range, the Bohlen family of Washington, D. C., spent the day skiing the backcountry. "It's exhilarating!" said Nina (in the lead). "It's physically demanding, and yet there's a rhythm, a flow, and a feeling of quiet awe amid all that grandeur."*

*Flares and fireworks streak the night as four hundred skiers snake down Aspen Mountain to the glittering town below. This torchlight descent highlights the annual Winterskol—a four-day festival of ski races, zany contests, and free-spirited fun. Diane Tegmeyer (above) served as co-director of the 1979 toast to winter. Opposite: After a strenuous day on the slopes, skiers soak tired bodies in one of the hot outdoor pools at Glenwood Springs.*

stunted. By the time we arrived at the fringe of the tree line, the stately, hundred-foot evergreens had shrunk to mere shrubs, distorted by wind and blowing snow.

Called krummholz, German for "crooked wood," these gnarled and twisted trees only inches high grew in the lee of boulders, which blunted the wind and allowed snow to accumulate and blanket the plants against the savagery of an alpine tundra winter. Fierce prevailing winds had pruned the branch buds on the windward side and fashioned the krummholz trees into pennant shapes. I saw them as brave banners of defiance with a wild, poignant beauty all their own.

We stepped out of the jeep well bundled up. Although patches of mist drifted down the slopes and scudding clouds cast distinct shadows, we carefully applied sunscreen lotion to our faces. The thin air, which retains 3°F. less heat for every thousand feet of elevation, also filters out the sun's rays less effectively. Twice as much ultraviolet radiation penetrates the atmosphere at 12,000 feet as at sea level.

A steady gale assailed us as we trooped after our instructor. Bettie showed us why building up soil is such a gradual process in this cold, windy, treeless environment. First, the elements slowly break up the bare rocks. Then pioneers like moss campion, with their webs of branches and tiny leaves, cover the ground and anchor the scant soil. As these cushion plants decay, they add organic material essential to other plants. Thus the pioneers represent the first stages of a progression that in several thousand years can turn barren, rocky terrain into the tundra's thick green turf.

Utterly absorbed, we stopped every few feet to peer at the clumps of cushion plants burgeoning with minuscule flowers. We also examined the various lichens—some puckered and spongy, some leafy or leathery—that had anchored themselves on the rocks or in the thin soil.

Then we noticed the sky was becoming ominous. One black-edged cloud after another spilled over the shoulders of the mountains and billowed upward, until they filled the sky. In the open landscape of the tundra, a human becomes a living lightning rod, so we abandoned all that prodigal beauty to avoid the fury of a summer thunderstorm.

SUDDEN STORMS occur often in summertime in the Rockies, but the weather was perfect the day I kayaked down Glenwood Canyon on the Colorado River. We were at the bottom of a deep valley, gliding along between near-vertical walls. The trip was the culmination of four afternoons of lessons for a class of rank beginners.

To me, comparing kayaking with canoeing is like comparing a motorcycle dash with a bus ride.

The glory of kayaking is the craft's high maneuverability. It can dart upstream, bank at high speed, surf on the crest of a wave, and dance down rapids—all this requiring a minimum of exertion and a maximum of deftness and skill.

The bane of kayaking is the kayak's instability. The boat requires balancing with hips, knees, and shoulders, and smooth, even strokes of the paddle. Sometimes it seemed as if just turning my head caused the kayak to spin out.

For four days I had floundered on a quiet, smooth stretch of the Roaring Fork just outside Aspen. Setting a straight course seemed the ultimate challenge. Every stroke turned the boat to one side or the other, and before I knew it, the kayak would pivot all the way around and I would be drifting downstream again, backward.

Peggy Ritzenberg of Bethesda, Maryland, an actress and a grandmother, had another problem. Her kayak had capsized the first day. "It hadn't occurred to me that if I turned over, I would be stuck in the kayak. The coldness of the water and the surprise of suddenly hanging upside down panicked me. Actually, when I stopped struggling, I fell right out of the boat," she told me. "The problem is, now I can't get over the fear of flipping over and being trapped underwater."

She sat there, staring at me. Then she thrust her chin forward, squared her shoulders, and paddled over to instructor Kirk Baker. "I think you'd better tip the kayak over,"

*Rocky Mountain bighorn sheep, partial to lofty heights, venture to lower elevations to forage in winter. Wildlife biologists have penned these in a 400-acre enclosure to test and treat them for lungworm. At right, pockets and channels of snow pattern the jumbled ridges of the Elk Mountains.*

she said, biting her lip. Moments later she came up with a triumphant smile.

Finally, after 20 hours of Kirk's patient instruction, we were ready for a river trip on the Colorado. Before I knew it I found myself in the hair-raising situation of lining up my kayak to shoot dead center of the rapids directly ahead.

Waves splashed over the bow. The boat dipped, rose, dipped again. Other waves angled in, threatening to knock the kayak sideways. Yet somehow Kirk's constant reminders to paddle with the whole upper body, like a swimmer doing the Australian crawl, stayed with me, and I managed to keep the kayak moving straight ahead and to hit the waves in the main current head on.

Suddenly the water was smooth and glistening, and there was time to marvel at the pink granite sculpture of the canyon walls.

I F I HAD NOT spent the time kayaking, perhaps I could have become a potter, a ballet dancer, or a glider pilot. Instruction in an amazing variety of skills is available in or near Aspen. Ballet West, a major dance company based in Salt Lake City, not only performs at Aspen but also runs a summer school at Snowmass Village, 12 miles away. Spectators gather to watch lithe dancers in leotards pirouetting in the shade of one of the school's free-form tent studios.

Downhill from the village, in a cluster of rustic log buildings of the Anderson Ranch Arts Center, master craftsmen teach ceramics, weaving, printmaking, woodworking, and photography to amateurs and professionals alike.

Still another school has found a home in Snowmass—the Aspen Academy of Martial Arts. Its dean, a serene and youthful man of 70, Marshall Ho'o, led me to the geodesic dome where students of the discipline of *T'ai chi ch'uan* were performing a sequence of postures with such evocative names as "white stork cools its wings" and "parting the wild horse's mane," developed in China more than a thousand years ago. Arms and legs, hands and feet and torso moved from one intricate pattern to another in graceful slow motion that looked a little like swimming through the air.

"In T'ai chi you learn to stand like a mountain and move like a river," Marshall said. "When you are anxious, your center of gravity rises to the shoulders, neck, face. That's where most tensions reside. By lowering your center of gravity and controlling your breathing, you begin to relax."

T'ai chi ch'uan, say its exponents, builds an inner confidence that fortifies a person to face a crisis or even an attack without panic. *Aikido,* a more vigorous martial art from Japan, also draws strength from serenity, relying on the concept of harmony rather than conflict in its techniques.

In a fascinating aikido demonstration, Tom Crum, president of the academy, showed how "yielding and harmonizing" can neutralize an attack. A colleague lunged and swung at him again and again; each time Tom deftly deflected or avoided the aggressor by blending with his movements. Eventually this would draw his opponent off balance, and then Tom would swiftly throw him.

Self-defense is also the basis of *hwarang do,* perhaps the most martial of the martial arts with a large repertoire of kicking techniques, including some spectacular spin kicks. It was developed by unarmed monks in Buddhist monasteries in Korea to combat marauders. Bob Duggan, a social scientist and martial arts instructor from California, was the first American to learn this esoteric system, which has been passed from teacher to disciple for more than 1,400 years.

"The traditional boxer swings from the upper body, but we get additional power by punching from the lower body as well," said Bob, retying the sash of his short, black-and-gray *do bak.* Hwarang do also uses joint-locks—turning a wrist, elbow, or shoulder in such a way that the weight of a finger is enough to immobilize an assailant with pain.

Still, my most vivid impression of the day was of the gentleness and quiet dignity of the people at the academy.

T HE SAME QUALITIES characterize Stuart A. Mace. For more than 30 years this botanist-artist-teacher has raised his voice in defense of animals and the abused, overgrazed land. With his longish graying hair, his craggy, handsome features weathered by sun and wind, and his passionately held convictions, he makes a compelling advocate of the environmental cause.

Mace lives 11 miles south of Aspen up the Castle Creek Valley, in a large log house he built himself. We wandered slowly across the high meadows nearby, where fiery blossoms of gilia, yellow alpine avens, blue harebells, and snowy clusters of broadleaf parsnip swayed in the breeze.

"It all starts right here—in this meadow, or a desert, or anywhere there is a single green plant. We couldn't exist without the ability of green plants to take sunlight, water, and the nutrients from the soil and turn them into food and energy," he said. "Since all of us are parasites of the green world, it's not so stupid, is it, to greet a plant as a friend, a brother, a sustainer? We are never going to achieve the brotherhood of man until we accept the brotherhood of all living things. All plants and animals have their place in the harmony and balance of nature."

For example, he said, the beavers, whose dams slow the spring runoff and store water so it can seep to underground aquifers. And the aspens, which help the land

*Summer on the Continental Divide finds snow still clinging to the heights while marsh marigolds bloom. Near Independence Pass, Annette St. Marie of California (above) faces the sunset to meditate before practicing the martial art of T'ai chi ch'uan.*

*Classical harmonies fill the evening air as students from the Aspen Music School give a recital on the patio of Toro's restaurant. In summer, music students play regularly at establishments along the mall—the brick-paved heart of Aspen lined with boisterous bars and discos, sophisticated boutiques, and elegant restaurants.*

recover after a forest fire by their role in building soil and providing vital shade for the young evergreens that eventually will take over.

Until recently, Stuart had another labor of love—caring for several dozen dogs and perpetuating the Eskimo art of dogsledding. He brought the furry malamutes and Eskimo and Siberian huskies back to Aspen from Alaska, where he had directed a dogsled operation that patroled, surveyed, and carried out rescue missions across the Arctic during World War II. Later he drove his teams in numerous episodes of the television series "Sergeant Preston of the Yukon."

Through Mace's efforts, Aspen has become one of the few places in the world that offer visitors the opportunity to travel by dogsled. Recently Stuart turned the dogs over to Dan MacEachen, who now continues the tradition at the Krabloonik Kennels near Snowmass.

There is little that compares with skimming across an empty, silent land on a frosty morning behind a swift team of dogs. Bundled snugly in several layers of blankets, while the chill winds blow and the beauty of winter glides by, I lapse into the most pleasant of reveries.

**M**OST WINTERS bring some 250 inches of snowfall to the slopes of Aspen's four ski mountains—a dry, powdery fluff that ignites a special longing in the hearts of thousands of skiers.

The streets are thronged with tanned, trim men and women in colorful, tight-fitting ski clothes; the après-ski bars resound to music, laughter, and sagas of the day's daring deeds; the restaurants—Swiss, Chinese, Mexican, Italian, Armenian—try to cope with the crowds; and in the discos, which come to life after 10 p.m., no one knows the time.

From mid-December to April, Aspen surrenders to the excitement and lighthearted revelry of winter and the sheer joy of swooping downhill.

After 78 years at the sport, Max Boté still feels no surfeit of skiing. Now, however, at 83, he waits for the clear bluebird days, when the snow and the vistas are dazzling. On such a morning, Max and I started up a series of four chair lifts at Aspen Highlands, a mile outside town.

"With the equipment nowadays, it's easy to learn to ski," said Max, pointing to our finely engineered fiberglass skis, our plastic, foam-padded ski boots, and our safety bindings designed to release the boot in a bad fall. "Back when I was skiing to kindergarten in Switzerland, we used long, hand-carved boards and tied them to our mountain boots with leather straps.

"We used skis for transportation. No one paid attention to form, yet we came down some *(Continued on page 128)*

*Rafts pitch and roll through churning Seidels (below) and Staircase Rapids on a day trip down the Arkansas River. "It was thrilling," said Carol Murray of Tucson, Arizona (at left, with visor), of her first experience with white-water rafting. "The water was freezing cold every time I got splashed in the face, but the weather was gorgeous and the company enjoyable. Yet even with five other people in the raft, I could still feel that I was alone in the wilderness, alone in the freedom of all outdoors."*

Against the scenic backdrop of the Rockies, future ballerinas study at the Ballet West summer dance school in Snowmass Village. Above, Yvonne Freant arranges wild flowers in Jeanette Marquez's hair before morning classes. While Penny McBrady changes from ballet slippers to toe shoes, Jeanette warms up at the barre. A Salt Lake City-based dance company in residence in Colorado for a six-week summer season, Ballet West contributes to Aspen's remarkably diverse schedule of events. In the 1940s Chicago industrialist Walter P. Paepcke, visualizing the quiet little town as a center of cultural and intellectual exchange, organized the Aspen Institute for Humanistic Studies and the Aspen Music School and Festival. Today, scholars and artists from around the world participate in the community's seminars, workshops, lectures, classes, ballets, and concerts.

125

*Colorado columbine
blooms in July, and a small
golden mantled ground
squirrel crouches shyly.*

*"The living world is a single, beautiful working entity," says*
*Stuart A. Mace, botanist, artist, teacher, and 32-year resident*
*of Ashcroft, as he discusses nature's complexities with*
*students of his class "Philosophy of the Green World."*

pretty grisly mountains," Max reminisced. Generally he spends little time looking back, and neither age nor nostalgia dims the luster of his smile or his azure eyes. But he can speak with rare authority: Included in his long skein of ski experiences are periods as an instructor with the Swiss Army during World War I and at Aspen Highlands' school after he retired from his engineering job in Indiana.

The lifts carried us upward past stately stands of spruce, their somber green gracing the vast white landscape. Below us we could watch the skiers on runs bulldozed through the thick forest. Many of them flashed by with the fluid grace that training and practice bring; others, rigid and awkward, labored ponderously and tentatively downhill.

"Skiing isn't something we do naturally," Max said. "On a steep slope, instinct tells us to lean back. But once we're back on our heels, the skis sail right out of control."

It took half an hour to reach our destination 11,475 feet up Loges Peak—just 200 feet from its summit. But it was the view, not the altitude, that took my breath away. Before following Max down the mountain, I paused for a long look. Gleaming white ridges and summits shaped the horizon, ascending so steeply they seemed to pierce the sky. Crests of Maroon and North Maroon Peaks—the Maroon Bells—and Pyramid Peak glistened against the blue heavens, and the lines of stratified rock were clearly defined by the snow.

THE PANORAMA graphically revealed the recent geologic history of this part of the Rockies. The bedded sedimentary rock so prominent in the famous Maroon Bells represents silt, clay, sand, and gravel carried by water rushing out of a long-lost mountain range, called by geologists the Ancestral Rockies. For some 50 million years, rivers pouring out of these mountains deposited the debris in a large inland sea. Then, about 65 or 70 million years ago, subterranean forces began pushing the sedimentary layers upward, and thrust to the surface huge blocks of the underlying granites and gneisses. Gradually the sea drained away from the uplifted land, and the Rocky Mountains emerged—a complex of mighty ranges extending 1,400 miles down the continent from northern British Columbia into New Mexico.

These mountains owe their present shape to the effects of an Ice Age that began about two million years ago. Massive glaciers left the beauty of today's landscape as marks of their passage—sharp pinnacles, great hollows called cirques, the faces of the peaks, the steep-walled U-shaped valleys.

The glaciers finally retreated about 10,000 years ago. But each winter brings mighty avalanches that roar down the steep slopes, bending and breaking trees, sweeping rocks in their path. Although Aspen itself is not threatened by

avalanches, many mountains in the area are scarred with the bald corridors, or chutes, that mark their paths. For people who ski fresh powder in backcountry where descents may have a pitch of 35° to 45°, avalanches are a deadly hazard. Nationwide, they take an average of 12 lives a year.

Tim Howe, avalanche-control supervisor for Aspen Mountain, is responsible for protecting skiers within the ski area. After a snowfall the ski patrol stabilizes the snow on the steep runs by skiing on it. "The friction of the skis melts and binds the snow. It's like embedding chicken wire in plaster; skiing holds the snow together," explained Tim.

He has seen and survived some awesome avalanches while skiing for his own pleasure in the backcountry. "There, when the tension in a snow slab is released—by skis, or even a chipmunk—it shatters like a piece of glass. There's a second or so after the fracture when the snowfield just stands still. It slowly starts moving, then accelerates to tremendous speed and force. It's like being caught in an ocean wave. A swimming motion helps to carry you to the top of the moving snow. But once the snow has settled, it is like concrete, and you can't move an eyelash.

"The heat and humidity of your breath tend to form an ice mask that seals off the air in the snow, so it's important to get a hand in front of your face to create as large an air pocket as possible as the slide comes to a stop.

"But time is of the essence in a rescue, because the

*Wrangler and partner scout the Elk Mountains as sunset fires the western sky. On popular supper rides at the Six Mile Ranch, just west of Aspen, residents and tourists enjoy a steak high in the mountains, take in the majestic scenery, then ride back by the light of the stars.*

FOLLOWING PAGES: *Colorful balloons take to the air in the Fourth Invitational Snowmass Hot Air Balloon Races, a two-day spectacle. The 1979 races, held at the Snowmass golf course, introduced "balloon golf." Each crew gets nine golf balls and, flying no closer than ten feet above the green, attempts a hole-in-one from the air.*

*Surrounded by the beauty and magic of the mountains, Aspen lies nestled in the Roaring Fork Valley, once the hunting ground of Ute Indians. The town lived high and prosperously from 1879 to 1893 after miners discovered silver in Aspen Mountain. Still a small community with a western flavor, Aspen enjoys boom times again—now as a mecca of cultural and recreational activities.*

PAUL CHESLEY

survival rate drops by 50 percent after only half an hour."

Our conversation was interrupted several times by a red telephone, signaling accident reports. The calls came from telephone boxes strategically located on the mountain. Each time, within seconds, two members of the patrol took off with a toboggan to carry the injured skier down.

"Most ski accidents occur in the afternoon on a clear, sunny day when everyone is on a high. They usually happen on a relatively flat slope, when the skiers are not paying much attention," said Tim.

What is the great attraction of skiing?

Jan Johannessen, a Norwegian who until the spring of 1979 headed the Snowmass Ski School, thinks that the sport adds an exciting element of risk lacking in our daily lives.

Others explain its appeal in other ways.

For former Texan Maco Stewart it fulfills dreams of flying, or moving with utter freedom. "With any sense of rhythm at all, you find yourself composing your own ballet."

"I don't care how cold it is," insists 10-year-old Nicole Goldman of Falls Church, Virginia, "as long as I can ski and don't have to walk down the mountain."

To Ed Lucks, who has been teaching the blind and disabled to ski ever since he started working with amputees from Viet Nam in 1966, there are the rewards of helping people to overcome severe handicaps. "So often my students tell me, 'If I can do this, I can do anything.' And they do."

Says Morris Purcel, electrical contractor of Macon, Georgia, "I enjoy this because it's just me and the mountain."

A S I RECALLED all those comments, I was resting in the languorous comfort of a heated therapy pool out of doors while tendrils of steam rose from the gently bubbling water to mellow the contours of Aspen Mountain and melt the snowflakes falling on my face.

Images of an Aspen winter drifted through my mind: The pearly light of early morning, with elk browsing on the white bark of aspens in a grove just beyond my window. The crackle of wood in a stove at a bookstore stocked only with books the owner thinks people *ought* to read. Exuberant skiers jostling for space at the bar while the setting sun ignites the summits with the fires of alpenglow. Cross-country skiing into a forest of snow-laden spruce at the beginning of night. Miner's headlamps lighting our path to the Pine Creek Cookhouse—a cabin of hand-hewn logs, where the savory paprika scents of a Hungarian dinner greeted us. And the reverent silence as we skied home by starlight.

A profusion of memories, a galaxy of remarkable people, an orbit of stimulating events trace the outlines of Aspen. But the beauty of the mountains reveals its heart.

# Las Sierras, los Volcanes

*Sunset tinges austere peaks of Mexico's Sierra Madre Oriental near the old silver-mining*

*By* GEORGE F. MOBLEY
*Photographed by the Author*

*center of Real de Catorce, in a harsh, semiarid region of the state of San Luis Potosí.*

*Shaped like a rough funnel, Mexico angles 2,000 miles from its northwestern to its southeastern border. The Sierra Madre Oriental, Sierra Madre Occidental, and Sierra Madre del Sur parallel the coastlines; in the interior lie the arid central plateau and northern mountains and basins. Along an east-west axis rises the Cordillera Neovolcánica, historic home of several advanced Indian cultures and site of early Spanish settlements. With more than two-thirds of the country mountainous, small Indian groups have survived in isolated enclaves little touched by modern life.*

MUD SLOSHED nearly to the axles of my four-wheel-drive pickup truck. Its headlights made little impression on the black gloom of the tunnel. Only the constant jouncing reassured me that somewhere beneath the ooze lay solid rock.

When I had first seen Mexico's Sierra Madre Oriental, the distant peaks appeared like phantom mountains, vague shapes half hidden by lowering curtains of desert rain along the monotonous road from Laredo, Texas, to Monterrey. Now, as the tunnel walls pressed close on both sides, the Sierra Madre was jarringly real.

The narrow roadway pierced the mountain at an elevation of 9,000 feet. The only light along the entire 1.2-mile passage was a single candle in a tiny chapel carved into the stone near one entrance. The candle burned in memory of the uncounted miners who died burrowing beneath this range.

Deep in the mountain, the tunnel widens and turns. It is the only spot where another vehicle can pass. But there was no other traffic. The creaking of trolleys laden with silver ore, the shouts and curses of mule skinners, all had long ago faded away.

Mountains dominate Mexico's landscape. Beginning just below the United States border, the Sierra Madre Oriental—Mother Range of the East—extends down the eastern side of Mexico, and the Sierra Madre Occidental down the western side. In the heart of the country a chain of volcanic peaks runs east and west. Beyond, broken terrain continues into neighboring Guatemala.

The eastern Sierra rises in waves of stone south of the Rio Grande's Big Bend and curves southeasterly for more than 750 miles. It was high on one of these stone waves in the state of San Luis Potosí that I finally emerged from the tunnel.

Before me, rocky slopes tumbled down on all sides to the junction of two deep canyons. Miles of crumbling stone walls lined the hills like forgotten sculpture. From the mountainside rose the ruins of Real de Catorce, once one of the wealthiest cities in all of New Spain.

Suddenly the silence was broken by the metallic clamor of bells. I drove along the steep stone street to the center of town, passed a handsome old church, and bounced to a halt in front of a sign proclaiming "Mesón de la Abundancia."

Through the massive doors of his restaurant, Higinio Gómez welcomed me as he poured cups of dark brown coffee. The building's thick walls and high beamed ceilings seemed burdened with the weight of history.

"This used to be the treasury," Higinio offered. He is tall, rugged, and self-assured. His grandfather came to Real de Catorce from Spain in 1875. His father was born next door in the house where Higinio now lives.

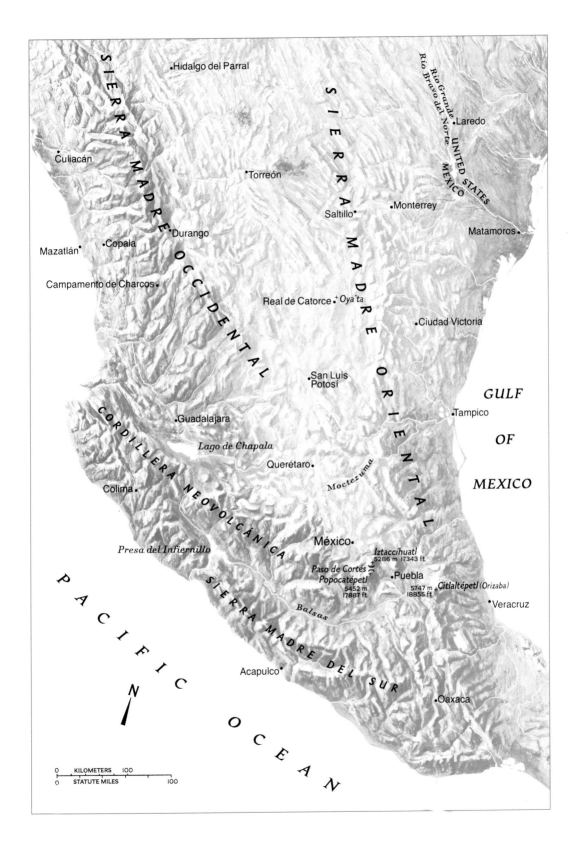

Hidalgo del Parral

SIERRA MADRE OCCIDENTAL

SIERRA MADRE ORIENTAL

Culiacán

Torreón

Río Grande
Río Bravo del Norte

Laredo

UNITED STATES
MEXICO

Saltillo

Monterrey

Durango

Matamoros

Mazatlán

Copala

Campamento de Charcos

Real de Catorce
+ Oya'ta

Ciudad Victoria

San Luis
Potosí

GULF

Guadalajara

Tampico

CORDILLERA NEOVOLCÁNICA

Lago de Chapala

Querétaro

OF

Colima

Moctezuma

MEXICO

Presa del Infiernillo

México

Iztaccíhuatl
5286 m  17343 ft

Paso de Cortés
Popocatépetl
5452 m
17887 ft

Puebla

Citlaltépetl (Orizaba)
5747 m
18855 ft

Veracruz

PACIFIC

SIERRA MADRE DEL SUR

Balsas

N

Acapulco

Oaxaca

OCEAN

0    KILOMETERS    100
0    STATUTE MILES              100

138

Crumbling ruins of a prosperous past surround the church and central plaza of *Real de Catorce*. *In the late 1800s a city of 40,000, now almost a ghost town with a population of about 500, Catorce sits high on a mountainside at 9,000 feet. With a gesture of invitation, José Luis Coronado (far left) sets out to harvest the fruit of the nopal cactus. Trudging up a cobblestone ramp, two children lug a heavy load of souvenirs to be sold in the plaza.*

"Catorce was a real city in those days," he said between sips of the steaming coffee. "Forty thousand people lived here. Now how many do we have? *¿Quién sabe?*— Who knows? Maybe 500, maybe 550.

"In 1773 prospectors found silver, and by 1779 there were more than a hundred mines. The city boomed in the 1800s. There were theaters, an opera, bullrings, a cockfight arena, gardens patterned after those of the haciendas of Spain. The wealthy could buy anything: the latest fashions, fine wines, and perfumes, all imported from Europe. Then, in 1910, came the Revolution, all the turmoil. With the richest ore gone, the mines soon closed and the people left."

Today Real de Catorce is slowly being rediscovered. Each year a few more tourists find their way to the nearly empty city. There are plans to pave the tunnel, and Higinio was busy converting the old treasury into a modern hotel.

He arranged a room for me across the patio from his own residence, while I wandered the cobbled streets of Catorce. All was peaceful, the silence broken only by the occasional braying of a burro, the laughter of children, a snatch of cheerful conversation. In front of the church, vendors were selling ripe red fruit of the nopal cactus, and candles to be offered by pilgrims who came to pray before a figure of St. Francis of Assisi. So renowned is the saint as a miracle worker that thousands of Mexicans travel to Real de Catorce every October for the fiesta in his honor.

Other pilgrims come to Catorce, too, for the surrounding area is sacred to Huichol and Tepehuan Indians. When I rejoined Higinio at the old treasury building, he had news for me. "I'm glad you're back," my host said. "There are Indians at Humberto's house."

HUMBERTO FERNANDEZ lived less than a block away. I found him and his guests seated in a central court, drinking coffee and chatting in low tones. The visitors were Tepehuans from an isolated area of southern Durango State in the Sierra Madre Occidental. They had come across Mexico on a pilgrimage to the legendary home of their ancestors' spirits near Real de Catorce.

They wore lightweight, loose-fitting shirts and trousers of white cotton, and broad-brimmed hats. Colorful blankets helped ward off the cold of the highlands.

Heading the group was Pedro Márquez Salvador, a slight man, straight and deeply bronzed. A shock of hair the color of dusty coal hung almost over his black eyes.

Pedro was a shaman, or spiritual leader, and he had brought five pilgrims to Catorce. They would spend the night in town and go next day to a mountain they called Oya'ta.

In the morning Pedro invited me to accompany them.

Heading eastward on an old mining trail, we climbed for three hours at a rapid, steady pace. Somehow I managed to keep up, partly because Pedro fell back to walk beside me, encouraging me with a gentle motion of his hand. He radiated a friendly warmth that seemed to give me strength. His sharp eyes, set in a face deeply weathered by a lifetime in the mountains, never missed a detail of our progress.

Near the summit, the trail turned steep and the wind turned fierce, sometimes blowing us off the path. When we reached the top, I sank to the rocky ground gasping for breath, but Pedro immediately set to work. He selected a flat spot partially sheltered from the wind by maguey plants and creosote bushes, swept it clean with a small shrub, and started a fire. His companions began to gather small tufts of grass. "It's for our animals back home," he explained. "Grass from the sacred mountain will bring them health and make their numbers multiply."

Sitting beside the fire, he pulled some resin and powdered red pigment from a small bag woven of brightly colored yarn. Until dark he worked the pigment into the resin, heating the mixture over the fire to make it pliable. Then he laid it aside until morning.

"Five times I have come to the mountain," Pedro said. "Twice I came by foot. It is a hard trip—a month each way."

Pushing close to the fire, ashes and smoke blowing in our eyes, we toasted tortillas over the coals for supper. Then, sheltering one another as best we could against the wind, we huddled together on the rocky ground for the night. I had a warm sleeping bag, but my companions slept each wrapped in a single blanket.

The wind howled, screamed, and roared, buffeting our precarious campsite. Rain came and went and came again.

Don Pedro had said we would stand facing the east at sunrise to begin the ceremonies. But instead of a sunrise, dawn brought only a mass of clouds streaming past our mountaintop. The icy wind showed no sign of abating. It seemed the gods had abandoned us to the demons of the storm.

No one moved until midmorning. Then, out of desperation, we built a fire. When my companions had tried to warm their bare feet near the meager flames, Pedro went about his work. To each of his companions he passed a slice of dried peyote. The bitter, hallucinogenic cactus is important in Tepehuan rites, and part of the pilgrimage would take the men into the desert for a new supply to carry home.

With the red resin prepared the night before, Pedro drew bright designs on ritual arrows made from slender stems of bamboo. The intricate work required nearly four hours.

Tiny ceremonial bowls of food were prepared. Then everyone sat around the fire, stuffed (Continued on page 146)

*"Dangerous to mess with," the white-sheathed spines of this low-growing cholla cactus cling tenaciously on contact. Red antenna-like spines three inches long frame buds of a barrel cactus. More species of cactus grow in Mexico than in any other country.*

141

Atop their sacred
mountain, Oya'ta, Tepehuan
Indians begin the ritual
for which they have
traveled 500 miles from
their home in the Sierra
Madre Occidental. After
they smoke pipes of strong
tobacco, the shaman
places a food offering with
four sacred arrows on a
maguey plant (below). One
pilgrim clutches dry grass
he will take home to his
animals to promote their
health and fertility.

PRECEDING PAGES: *After a long night on the mountain, Tepehuan pilgrims hurry down an old mining road to Catorce, with only their blankets as wraps against a biting cold wind.*

pipes carved from deer antler with a strong tobacco the men called *magoche,* and smoked.

When the pipes grew cold, Pedro faced east and voiced a lengthy prayer in his native tongue. The tiny bowls of food were passed over the body of each individual in a rite of purification, then were placed among the leaves of a young maguey with four of the sacred arrows. Just as this offering was presented, the clouds parted to reveal the mountains around us. Far below, sunlight flooded the valley.

We packed our few possessions and raced down the mountain, blankets whipping in the wind. The sky closed again. A gray mass swept upward from the west, and we arrived back at Real de Catorce in late afternoon cold and soaked with rain. Throughout the night and into the next day, the storm continued to rage.

When the wind finally came to rest and the sun returned, the six Tepehuans and I climbed into my pickup truck and nosed down a burro trail cut in the wall of a precipitous canyon. We paused at a cave in the canyon wall long enough for Pedro to fill several bottles with sacred water. By sunset we had reached the desert plain and settled in for the night at one of the infrequent stations on a lonely stretch of track of the Laredo-to-Mexico City railroad.

The seven of us dined on 25 cents' worth of tortillas—all the village had to offer until morning—and lay down for an uneasy sleep intermittently disrupted by the roar of passing trains only a few yards away.

There are roads of a sort in this dry region, cobwebs of dust that radiate irregularly from the tiny villages along the railroad. In the morning we followed one of these. After about two hours, we eased to a stop under a lone tree.

With a degree of tension and excitement I hadn't observed before, Pedro prepared several more ceremonial arrows. The Tepehuans believe the peyote cactus plants are tracks of the *venado,* the sacred deer of their mysticism. The venado hides his tracks well. The inconspicuous little cactus grows with its top barely flush with the ground, often sheltered under a creosote bush. Its dusty gray-green color serves as an efficient camouflage.

We spread out and walked a couple of miles across the desert before a whistle from Pedro brought us all together.

"The first," Pedro said, plunging an arrow into the ground beside the tiny cactus—thus, he explained, trapping the spirit of the sacred deer and assuring a good harvest. Soon another was found. It, too, was marked by an arrow.

A shout went up. A clump of seven had been found.

"It's a good omen," Pedro said, marking the clump with three arrows. Squeezing juice from one of the growing plants with the tip of another arrow, he carefully drew designs on the wrists of his companions. Then, in a sacrament of reverence and dignity, he passed slices of fresh peyote down the cheeks of his followers and placed them in their mouths. In turn, he too ate a slice. The rest of the day was spent harvesting the cactus, cutting the plants carefully just below the surface of the soil so they would regenerate from the roots.

That night we camped on the desert, ate our tortillas around a creosote-bush fire under a canopy of brilliant stars, and slept to the music of yapping coyotes. Next day the harvest was good. The peyote was cleaned, baskets were carefully packed, and I offered to drive my friends to their home in Durango State. Pedro recovered his arrows and anointed the clump of seven peyote plants with sacred water from the cave. Then he placed a small wooden cross on the ashes of our campfire, and we left.

TWO DAYS LATER we turned off the highway and headed south into wild mountains on a tortuous logging road. "It's only about three hours' drive," Pedro insisted. "We can almost see the village now." After seven hours we arrived, exhausted and dusty, battered by the rocky trail. Campamento de Charcos looked like an early western logging camp. Wooden huts were scattered haphazardly over a bleak, rocky knoll. Blue wood smoke drifted lazily from stovepipes in the gathering dusk.

"We will remain here for several days," Pedro said. "Then we'll get burros to take us on to our home farther back in the mountains. Tonight, we will stay with friends."

It was dark when we found the house. It sat in a clearing in the pine forest some distance from the lumber camp. Pedro led us into a tiny room. A woman knelt beside a stove—a simple adobe frame with a slightly bowed sheet of metal on top—and ground corn on a stone *metate*. She was nearly lost in the darkness. Only the glow of coals in the stove and the dim light of a candle outlined her form. Bent over the metate, she seemed as timeless as the mountains.

The woman cooked tortillas on the top of the stove and passed them to us. Then she scrambled an egg and handed it to me. I rolled it in a tortilla and ate it slowly. It was very special.

"I am sorry," she apologized, "but we are poor."

In the night it rained. When I awoke, the woman again was bent over her stone, steadily grinding corn. She had already mopped up the rain that had come through holes in the roof; and she had brought water from a distant spring, balancing it in a large container on her head.

With a deep sense of melancholy, I said goodbye to my companions. Only Pedro went to the lumber camp with me. Satisfied that I was on the right road, he left. I turned north and began the long drive back to the highway.

*From the mountaintop, the Tepehuans descend to the desert to gather peyote for their mystic ceremonies. With a sacred arrow dipped in cactus juice, the shaman traces a pattern on each pilgrim's wrist. A day's labor yields several baskets of peyote buttons, cleaned and packed for the trip home.*

Once on the main road, I drove west into a region of tortured mountain canyons. As the road plunged toward the coast, tropical vegetation replaced the pine and oak forest.

Shortly after banana leaves appeared among the foliage, I turned onto the gravel road to Copala, a hamlet nestled low on the western flank of the mountains. Friends had insisted that I see Copala, and I looked forward to a couple of days' rest among the bougainvilleas and hydrangeas.

I pulled into a small campground and, to my surprise, was greeted in English.

"Welcome to Copala!" The voice belonged to Daniel Garrison, who owns the campground and serves an excellent Mexican lunch to visitors. I sampled his tacos, enchiladas, chiles rellenos, and frijoles, and in the coolness of the rustic restaurant felt the tensions of the mountain drive fade away.

I commented on how exhausting the trip from Durango was. "A friend of mine counted the curves once," Daniel replied. "He told me there are more than 3,300.

"My mother came over those mountains from Durango with her parents when she was four years old. There was no road then. It took three weeks by burro. They brought their cattle and all their possessions with them."

We went for a stroll, and climbed a hill overlooking the village. Corn had grown there on a slope so steep we wondered how the farmer had avoided sliding right off his field.

"When the rain comes," Daniel said, "there's always a flood of mud down the valley. But in two years, you will never know this hill had been cleared. They will clean off another field for next season's crop, and won't touch this one again for several years."

Back at Daniel's home, we sat on the terrace under a towering *haba* tree as evening approached. Flocks of green parrots winged overhead, bound for the night's roost. A screeching pair of colorful macaws climbed down from the roof, ambled across the terrace, and settled on a railing next to where we sat. "That's Pascual and Romana," Daniel said. "They were both wild, but someone shot them down. They are well now, but their wings were broken and they can't fly. They are fairly tame, but be careful. They can bite."

Daniel told me he had returned to Copala after a long absence. "I worked in the oil fields in the States for 11 years," he said. "I worked like a dog and hadn't saved a cent to show for it, so I sold my Corvette and my house and came back here. I still don't have any money, but I'm happy. I don't work so hard, and when I do I see the results."

He lit a kerosene lantern. We sat and talked in its warm glow while his wife, Chalva, baked a papaya pie.

Pascual and Romana had ceased their raucous quarreling and had gone to roost. We sat immersed in the stillness for a long time, listening for the tentative songs of the evening's first crickets.

"Copala is bound to change," Daniel said. "More and more people come here each year. Someday we'll have electricity and television, but for now I'm content."

The pie was ready. We sampled it hot from the oven, rich and delicious, its sweet aroma blending with the fragrant scents of the tropical night.

VOLCANIC PEAKS tower over the heart of Mexico, and far underground seethe perpetual lakes of molten rock. Here at the 19th parallel the country is slashed from the Pacific Ocean to the Gulf of Mexico by deep geological fractures. Lava boiling up from subterranean cauldrons has created mountain giants with heights unsurpassed by anything between Canada and South America. The three highest of these volcanos are crowned year-round with glacial ice.

For thirty years I had longed to see these giants. For me they were magic mountains, peaks with mysterious names like Popocatépetl, Iztaccíhuatl, Citlaltépetl. They were revered by the Aztecs and the ancient peoples that preceded them.

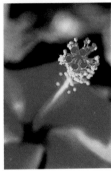

In Mexico City I met Alfredo Careaga, a strong and gentle man of 47. A long-time member of the Club de Exploraciones de México, he has climbed more than a thousand mountains in Mexico, Guatemala, and the United States.

Soon we had left the smog and congestion of Mexico City behind, passed an assortment of volcanic cones and craters that dot the Valley of Mexico, and were driving a well-paved road upward through fragrant pine forests. Where the steep climb eased into a broad pass, we slowed to a halt.

The late evening sun rouged the rugged rock walls of Iztaccíhuatl, "White Woman," north of us, and glinted off the glaciers of classic Popocatépetl, "Smoking Mountain," to the south. A cold wind spilled across the pass, hissed through coarse clumps of *zacatón* grass, and buffeted a simple monument erected to mark the spot where a renegade Spanish officer with a few hundred soldiers passed into the Valley of Mexico in 1519 to conquer Moctezuma and the Aztec empire. We were standing in the Paso de Cortés.

"Let me tell you the legend of Popocatépetl and Iztaccíhuatl," Alfredo said. "Popo was a warrior of a Nahuatl tribe, and Izta was the daughter of the chief. Popo and Izta fell in love. Izta's father said he would consent to their marriage, but Popo first would have to conquer an enemy tribe. When Popo returned with the head of the enemy chief, he would find a festival prepared to celebrate his victory and his marriage to Princess Iztaccíhuatl.

"So Popo went to war; but when he returned with the

*Brightly hued fauna and flora of tropical forests grace the lower Pacific slopes of the Sierra Madre Occidental: a military macaw against a backdrop of banana leaves, and yellow-centered scarlet hibiscus.*

FOLLOWING PAGES:
*Almost hidden amid lush vegetation, tiny Copala lies comfortably between the warm Pacific coastal lowlands and the chill heights of the Sierra Madre Occidental.*

head of his enemy, he learned that Izta had died. Grief-stricken, Popo took the body of the beautiful princess, carried her to a high mountain, and laid her on the crest. This is the form of the reclining woman we can see today.

"Then Popocatépetl put fire to a torch and stayed to watch over the sleep of Iztaccíhuatl. That is why we often see smoke rising over Popocatépetl."

Alfredo and I watched from the Paso de Cortés as the sun slipped into the haze off to the west. For a moment the snowy torch of Popocatépetl blazed anew with reflected sunlight; then night settled over the great volcanic plateau.

We found refuge at a modern, comfortable lodge at Tlamacas, on the flank of Popocatépetl. We agreed to walk up to the glaciers the next morning, and retired early.

Well before sunrise we set out, but the weather was bad. Stiff winds drove volcanic dust and sand into our eyes. The trail was like a steep uphill climb on sandy beach in the thin air of 14,000 feet. Furthermore, I had awakened at midnight with a throbbing headache that refused to go away.

"Mal de montaña," Alfredo said. Altitude sickness.

We pushed on until we reached the first traces of snow, then paused to rest at a small mound of stones arranged high on a ridge in ages past by Indians who came here to worship.

Nausea swept over me. With that sensation added to the throbbing in my head, I realized my enthusiasm for the sacred heights of the Aztecs was on the wane.

"Technically, Popocatépetl is an easy climb," Alfredo said. "Sure, falling rocks are always a danger. The lava is crumbly, and sometimes rocks come down like bullets. And the ice can be a problem. But the thin air at such a height—the summit is nearly 18,000 feet—is the worst danger. Too many people who come to climb Popo run serious risks because they don't take time to prepare themselves."

Reluctantly, we returned to the lodge and drove to a lower elevation.

Back in Mexico City, we picked up Alfredo's son, also called Alfredo, and headed for Citlaltépetl, or Pico de Orizaba—at 18,855 feet Mexico's highest mountain.

Alfredo the younger is an astrophysicist who had just completed two months of exhausting studies in computer science. He was ecstatic about spending a weekend in the mountains. I asked how long he had been a climber.

"I was born climbing," he laughed. "I made my first trip up a mountain at six weeks of age in a rucksack on my mother's back, and I've been climbing ever since."

Volcanic Pico de Orizaba overlooks the southern highlands of the Sierra Madre Oriental. We drove up through pine forests onto a high ridge, the overheated engine of my pickup struggling in the rarefied air. Near road's end we

CNEP
117

parked beneath the white mass of Mexico's biggest glacier, savored the grandeur around us, and set up camp.

Stars were already appearing over the icy form of Orizaba. While we ate sandwiches of rich Oaxaca cheese, Alfredo the son drew upon his knowledge of astronomy to point out Sirius and Canopus, the planets Jupiter and Saturn, the constellations Leo and Orion.

And he talked about his affection for the mountains.

"They are my friends," he said. "Each has its own personality. There are special mountains I visit when I'm happy, or when I'm sad, mountains I visit when I remember friends that have perished climbing.

"I grew up in the mountains. They are home to me, and I take personal offense when I see them abused by pollution or by practices that lead to erosion.

"We live in a beautiful universe. The closest we can come to touching the stars—those of us who are not aviators or astronauts—is in the mountains."

It was night now, and the stars seemed to close around the crown of Orizaba. And then I remembered. Of course. In the ancient language of the Aztecs, the name for Pico de Orizaba was Citlaltépetl—mountain of the stars.

*Residents of Copala enjoy a light moment as a youngster tests the patience of a yearling bull in a tug-of-war. Here on the moist, fertile western slopes, life comes easier than in the higher country, where farmers must cope with thin soil and a short growing season.*

*Awesome volcanic giants rise to heights of more than 17,000 feet through the mists of surrounding valleys. Snow-covered much of the year, Iztaccíhuatl or White Woman (foreground) and Popocatépetl, Smoking Mountain, inspired an ancient legend of love and tragedy. Popo still spews occasional smoke and steam from its crater (right).*

FOLLOWING PAGES: *As daylight creeps over the mountains, veteran climber Alfredo Careaga the elder ascends the steep slope of Popocatépetl.*

# The Great Smokies

*Islands in a foaming sea, the tops of the Great Smoky Mountains jut above surflike clouds.*

*By* CHARLTON OGBURN
*Photographed by* JAMES P. BLAIR

*Most of the range lies within the boundaries of the United States' most visited national park.*

"THE OLD DAYS was much the best." Birgie Manning was shyly recalling her girlhood in Greenbrier Cove, Tennessee—a girlhood that, despite her 73 years, lives still in her candid, steady, blue-gray eyes.

"There was good schools and good churches," Birgie explained. Yet these, I could tell as she and her husband talked in their present home at nearby Emerts Cove, were really symbols of something more; the two-room school she had attended could hardly have been superior to today's facilities. Johnnie Manning's face had a glow of satisfaction with life, but an extra sparkle came to his eyes when he spoke of the near-independence once provided by local crops —corn, beans, potatoes, apples; or the singing schools most people went to ("the best singing in the world"); or his annual boyhood trip to Knoxville, camping beside the wagon.

"It was a healthy life," said Glenn Cardwell as he escorted my wife, Vera, and me to see some of the people who had lived in the Great Smoky Mountains before the national park came. "My mother never took us to a doctor. She treated us with medicinal plants. Every spring she'd line up all nine of us and dose us with wormwood tea. It was horrible. 'Take it like a man,' she'd say."

Glenn was born in Greenbrier Cove himself, and is now a park ranger with a protective, half-filial regard for the old-timers. His mother is an Ogle—and it was an Ogle who about 1805 settled White Oak Flats, today's Gatlinburg, located on the Tennessee side of the mountains and now the northwestern gateway to the park.

Off to the south we could see the crest of 6,593-foot Mount Le Conte rising more than a mile above us. To me it is the most dramatic mountain in the eastern United States, with its storm-raked, prowlike summits commanding views of almost all the 6,000-footers in the Smokies. The central and highest part of the range's backbone ridge—68 miles long by the Appalachian Trail—is capped at 6,643 feet by Clingmans Dome. Great Smoky Mountains National Park, 808 square miles, encompasses almost the entire range. Relocation of the inhabitants began soon after the park authorization bill was passed by Congress in 1926, and was in full tide by 1930 when the park officially came into existence. But since many were granted life tenancy, some occupation has continued to the present.

Birgie Manning's forebears had lived in Greenbrier Cove, at the foot of Le Conte, back to the time of her great-grandparents, whose photograph she showed us. "I've seen seven generations of our family," she said.

Continuity: That, in addition to self-sufficiency, I learned, was an aspect of the past that was greatly valued. Family portraits on the wall tend to be a feature of mountain

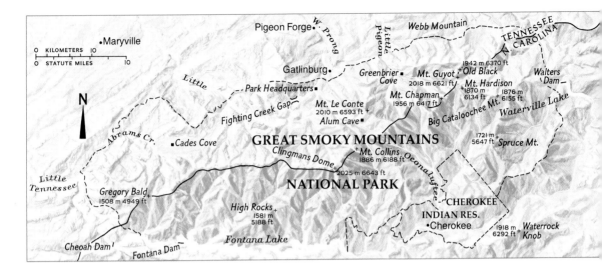

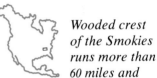

homes. At the Mortons', between Webb Mountain and the park, seven were hung in the form of a family tree. Among them was a photograph of Verless Morton—now 88 and nearly deaf—in World War I uniform and quite recognizable by his aquiline nose. The Army has always drawn first-rate soldiers from these mountains.

Albums of family photographs were brought out for me by Verless's son Henry, who would inherit land his great-grandparents had owned. Meanwhile, he was "pastoring" the Baptist church down the road. Verless had been a surveyor in the Smokies in the days before the park, and told me he had broken both legs twice on the job; one double break was caused by a boulder that rolled down on him.

"He's such a gentle-looking man," I said to my companion, Olin Watson, as we left. "Well," said Olin, who was born on Two-mile Branch near the present park headquarters, "there was a time when nobody was readier with a gun. He had to be. He was quite a card player, and carried a good deal of money on him. At Christmas he used to take an upper room in the old Market House in Knoxville and scatter a couple of hundred dollars in coins out the window."

Verless Morton's story was a variant on a mountain tradition, by which dependable if unauthorized profits came out of a vat through a copper coil. From Cades Cove, today a much-visited part of the park, you could see the smoke of a hundred stills, wrote the regional historian Joseph S. Hall. He was quoted to me by Ralph Lawson, a distinguished-looking scion of the Sparks family once prominent in the cove. "Mother was indignant at the charge," Ralph said. "But I told her that just maybe the writer wasn't lying. Then I ticked off 12 members of the family *(Continued on page 168)*

*(Continued on page 168)*

*Wooded crest of the Smokies runs more than 60 miles and reaches heights above 6,600 feet. A sturdy breed of mountain folk once lived in this rugged region. Today Great Smoky Mountains National Park encompasses 517,368 acres of forested wilderness threaded by 800 miles of scenic trails. Abandoned cabins and restored communities, such as Cades Cove, recall the pioneer days. On the Cherokee Indian Reservation just southeast of the park live descendants of the area's earlier inhabitants.*

*Enveloped in morning mist, two deer browse below ghostly ridges rising from Cades Cove, where dewdrops make pearly strands of a spiderweb on a barbed-wire fence. One of the moving spirits behind Great Smoky Mountains National Park, Horace Kephart, prophesied: "It will be a joy and a wonder to our people for all time." More than 6,600 parcels of land passed from private to public domain to establish the park. Some of the residents, like Uncle Lem Ownby (opposite), retained lifetime leases on their property. Now only Uncle Lem remains—91 years old and blind, but still tending bees beside his small, tin-roofed house near Jakes Creek.*

PRECEDING PAGES: *Agleam with autumn gold, tulip trees frame a restored split-rail fence and a shingled relic of the early 19th century. In this log cabin lived John and Lurena Oliver, first permanent settlers of Cades Cove, a snug valley nestled among wooded ridges. The rich forests of the Smokies, especially the stands of huge tulip trees, or yellow poplars, attracted a thriving timber industry. In the 1920s the logging and sawmill operations produced millions of board feet of lumber. Fire and erosion followed the heavy logging. With the coming of the park, the woodlands began a long, slow comeback still in progress.*

Slowly turning wheels of a mule-powered mill fed by Clifford (Pete) Tipton press sorghum cane in a syrup-making demonstration at Cades Cove. From the white-oak barrel with its tow-sack strainer, the cane juice goes into evaporating pans over wood fires. Orville and Grace Clabo of Sevierville, Tennessee, skim the sweet, hot syrup. At right, a young visitor savors a sampling from a pan, as mountain children must have done every autumn for more than a century.

who turned out a good whiskey." At one time the hamlet of Cosby, only three miles from the northeastern boundary of the park, was called the moonshine capital of the world.

With Olin, president of the Smoky Mountain Historical Society, we took the road up Fighting Creek to Little River. In these mountains, the few roads follow streams where possible. Along the valleys and up the sheltered slopes extends the great cove forest, in which red oaks, white ashes, basswoods, and sugar maples reach maximum height, and tulip trees—here called yellow poplars—sometimes rise as high as a five-story building before branching. Rhododendrons 20 feet tall may keep all but a few weak beams of sunshine from the brook below, and usually the only sound is the mellow converse of the waters. Of the primeval forest, as much as 40 percent remained when the park came to save it.

I asked how many private homeowners remained in the park. "Just Uncle Lem Ownby," said Olin. "He's the last one. He's 91 and blind."

At a cabin on Jakes Creek, we crossed a dooryard swarming with bees from 20-odd hives. "Up until about 15 years ago I had 145, and the yield from the biggest would fill two 32-pound cans," Uncle Lem said. The bees found plenty of nectar in the woods, from basswood, yellow poplar, and sourwood. Bowed with age but still sturdy-looking, he had a face almost unlined. When I remarked on that, "I lay it to the honey," he said. "Or the good mountain air," said Olin.

While Vera took in the neatness of the cabin's spare interior, we listened to the flow of reminiscence.

"Jasper Mellinger stopped by here for breakfast, and it was the last anyone saw of him for seven years. His skeleton was found then, with a pocketknife and some change. It was said he stepped in a bear trap, whose I won't say. But there were other stories, too. Of course, bear traps have been illegal a long time. Someone I also won't name got caught setting one. When the judge handed down a fine, he said, 'I got that right here in my pocket.' The judge said, 'I'm giving you a year and a day, too. You got that in your pocket?' "

". . . there was another boy about my age, 7 or 8, and we were out hunting possum in the woods one night with a broke-down foxhound when that hoot owl started up. We knew what it was, but we broke and ran anyway!"

". . . when he hauled the bear out of the trunk of his car and the cow got its scent, she cleared three strands of barbed wire. As for the goat, they never did find it."

All the tales! They keep the past alive, and suffuse it with a special charm. But if the past awakens nostalgia among these mountain folk, the chief reason is one that Johnnie Manning suggested when he said, "If a family's cow was dry, they never lacked for milk as long as a neighbor's was giving." Bob Wear of Cades Cove made the same point. Bob is a descendant of Col. Sam Wear, who built Fort Wear at Pigeon Forge, six miles north of Gatlinburg, in the 1780s. "If a family's house burned down, the neighbors turned to and put up another. If a man got sick, they tilled his crops."

Strikingly, I heard almost identical words from an ancestral foe of the people I had been talking with. He was Utsvdv Tsiladoosgi—translated Goingback Chiltoskey—a Cherokee born in 1907, as was Bob Wear. "G. B." lives in a modern house he designed himself on the reservation of the Eastern Band of Cherokee, which abuts the North Carolina side of the national park on the southeast; but his wood carving has made him known far beyond the reservation borders.

I HAD SOME MISGIVINGS about visiting a man whose people my forefathers had tried to expunge from their homeland—succeeding to such extent that only about a thousand had escaped the forced march over the "Trail of Tears" to Oklahoma in 1838-39 by hiding out deep in the Smokies. The imposing mien of the patrician awaiting us did not entirely reassure me. But he had long ago come to terms with my world. His wife, Mary Ulmer Chiltoskey, is in fact white, a native of Alabama. She is also an animated, articulate expositor of Cherokee traditions. While she told Vera about the class in Cherokee cooking she was soon to give to college students, G. B. told me that he had gone from the reservation school to high school in Greenville, South Carolina, supporting himself by woodworking. After graduating from Haskell Institute in Kansas, he taught in Indian schools.

"In 1942 I went to work at Fort Belvoir, near Washington, constructing models for the Army Corps of Engineers. From 1946 to '54 I had other jobs, mostly teaching; then I returned to Belvoir until 1966. I was very glad to retire so that I could carve as a hobby." Today he can't keep up with the orders for the lifelike figures he creates, human and animal.

Chiltoskey has not forgotten the tragedy of his ancestors. "But you can't live in a world of a hundred years ago," he said. "You've got to make a living in this one." That necessity has sent the young people of the reservation out to factories and government jobs, all but dooming the spirit of community he so misses. Yet all is not gone. His wife reminded him of the friends—more than 20—who came to offer help to a sick neighbor. And there are other links with the old days. "If it were necessary, Berdina Crowe next door knows how to feed her family for a week on wild plants growing within a hundred yards." Goingback's own work—a heron of pale buckeye, a little bear of dark cherry burl, perfect down to its tiny teeth—evoke the ancient affinities of the Cherokee, as the lineaments of the artist's remarkable

*Pigments of fall paint a blazing sumac from the bottom up. Glorious in their autumn foliage, the Smokies also brighten with color in spring and summer, displaying more than a thousand kinds of flowering plants. In June and July, rhododendrons and mountain laurels flaunt their spectacular bloom.*

face evoke ten thousand years of North American history.

That morning we had come over the Smoky Mountains' chill heights, past forests still not fully leafed out on the summer solstice, and had wound down slopes where the Cherokee bands starved 150 years ago. The pathos of their memory merged in my mind with that of their white successors buried in a cemetery in the woods above Greenbrier Cove—one of 130 in the park—with touching little gravestones, irregular slabs of native rock, painfully chiseled. For me it was a day when the past was very much present.

But in the southern Appalachians it always is. Certainly it is for the scientists. They look back 250 million years or more to the elevation of this range in what geologists theorize was the slow collision of North America and Africa. "Subsequent erosion has left a deep cover of rich, moist soil," said Dan Pittillo, plant ecologist of Western Carolina University. "That, the hospitable climate, and the variety of habitats for mixed flora have resulted in a greater diversity of plant life—more than 1,700 species—than any other area this size in the temperate zone of North America."

Of bryophytes alone—mosses and liverworts—"there are almost as many species in one gorge of the Blue Ridge as in all of California," said Lewis Anderson of Duke University, whom I met at the Highland Biological Station. Throughout the Smokies are found more than 400 kinds of bryophytes, Aaron J. Sharp of the University of Tennessee told me.

The two men emphasized that ever since the beginning of flowering plants—a period paleobotanists reckon to be at least 135 million years—the southern Appalachians have been available for plant colonization. And the Smokies, with their variety of habitats, are the quintessential Appalachians. It was from these mountains that the lowlands to the east and south were vegetated as they emerged from the sea; and from the Smokies that, much later, the forests of beech, yellow birch, sugar maple, spruce, and fir repossessed the northlands upon the retreat of the ice sheet that had laid waste two-thirds of the continent. Those forests still mantle the high Smokies, whose summits stand dark with several of the same conifers that ring Canada's glacial lakes.

Dr. Sharp and Dr. Anderson spoke, too, of the similarities between southern Appalachian and southeast Asian flora, which the former had studied in Japan. "Dr. Sinske Hattori and I found some examples extending even to the Himalayas," he said.

The explanation lies in the vast forest that once extended from the Appalachians to the Himalayas by way of a land bridge across what is now the Bering Strait. But the southern Appalachians were already ancient when the dinosaurs disappeared and the kingdom of seed-bearing plants first emerged. To the imaginative eye, the wraiths of condensing vapor that have given the Smoky Mountains their name are the mists of an inconceivable antiquity.

In the summer of 1979, Dr. Sharp and Dr. Anderson climbed Le Conte to observe its rich northern flora. An 11-mile round trip, including an ascent of 2,700 feet, wasn't a bad walk for a man of 75; but then Dr. Sharp has been hiking the Smokies for 50 years. The route they took follows liquid-diamond streams, passes under the massive rock overhang of Alum Cave, and skirts cliff faces so sheer a hand cable has been stretched along the trail so it can be negotiated safely. The same hike acquired for me the character of a pilgrimage when it disclosed a huge ridge far above me mantled by dark spruce forest: a presiding presence ribbed by buttresses so steep no man, I suspect, had ever set foot on them, and little could cling to their crests except catawba rhododendron which mottled them with a profusion of pink bloom. To me it was the epitome of the natural earth's nobility and wild beauty.

In dappled woods, a small creek courses musically among ancient boulders. Abundant highland rainfall feeds more than 750 miles of streams throughout the park, but the Smokies have no natural lakes or ponds. Five man-made reservoirs, including Fontana Lake on the park's southwestern border, collect the constant flow of water.

**B**ACKPACKERS COME to the Smokies to savor a wilderness little changed since the red man first saw it—and they come in such numbers that, to protect that wilderness, overnight camping privileges must be rationed. Yet they are a small portion of the eight to nine million vacationers a year that visit the park and adjacent Gatlinburg, with its 200 motels. Most see no more of the Smokies than their car windows bring into view; yet they must feel that here they come into significant touch with the aboriginal continent.

"Tourism gives employment to about 25 percent of our young people," Glenn Cardwell told me. "The rest we lose." But Glenn's cousins have inherited at least a remnant of the old-time mountains. Their father, the late Ezra Ogle, used the money he got for his land within the park to buy a hollow at Boogertown, east of Pigeon Forge. "He had big offers for it, but he wouldn't sell," Glenn said.

The Ogle house is a mountain home for sure, board-sided and unpainted under a steep shake roof with the porch side hung from top to bottom with bits of hardware. When I visited the owner shortly before his death, he was bent just enough by his 81 years to pass comfortably beneath the ceiling beams. We talked of old-time logging, which provided many families with sorely needed cash and left the Smokies with miles of railway beds now overgrown. Ezra Ogle recalled yellow poplars that required a 10-foot saw, and chestnut logs nearly as thick that were dragged in 12-foot lengths by "cattle"—oxen—to the railroad. "Dry chestnut was very desirable for stills, because it didn't make much smoke," he said. "A lot of chestnut fence rails disappeared."

*Riding a white mule, Pete Tipton, descendant of Cades Cove pioneers, passes the blacksmith shop, one of the National Park Service exhibits. Below, splashed with autumn hues, mountainsides glow near the cove, where the first Tiptons settled in the early 1800s. Opposite, tobacco farmer George Franklin, like his hardy mountain forebears, still works the land at 74. In his barn near Emerts Cove, he grades the golden-leafed crop.*

To talk with another veteran of mountain life, we drove to the northwestern foothills. Vera and I found Opal Myers working in her vegetable patch near the end of a gravel road. We accompanied her past chickens, guinea fowls, and a lame red coonhound up a ramp of planks into her house. Passing between a washtub of unshucked corn and jars of deep purple contents, we entered a museum of mountain artifacts. "I let the pokeberries boil too long and had to make jelly," she said of the purple jars. Pokeberry juice (not the seeds or skins, which are poisonous) was for arthritis. For coughs, "you take chestnut leaves; inner bark or root of red alder, yellow willow, white pine, wild cherry, and hemlock tree; life-everlasting, which is rabbit tobacco; and mullein. Cook together in a big kettle, drain off the juice, and add sugar."

Good-humored as a dumpling, ever smiling, Opal told us about a lifetime in the mountains. "I was born right under Halls Top and was brought up at Ebenezer Mission, which has since burned down. I went away to a Presbyterian boarding school in Kentucky, then to Milligan College in Johnson City, always working, of course. Times were so bad my parents couldn't afford a two-cent stamp to write to me.

"From 1933 to 1973 I taught—for the first 22 years in a one-room schoolhouse, walking five miles round trip every day. I had as many as 62 children—all eight grades. In the Depression we had one book for 20 first-graders."

Opal Myers discovered early that handicapped children, up to then kept at home, usually did well if taught right along with their fellows—something most educators have only recently come to realize. In the 1960s she was the model for a character in Catherine Marshall's novel *Christy*. Now at 69, while bringing up two grandsons, she looks forward to new labors in a mission for orphans to be built nearby.

I asked Opal how mountain people differ from others. "They're friendlier and far healthier," she replied. "And 'work-brickle,' my mother called it—they can do any job."

Opal's brother is prospering in California; so, in Connecticut, is her comely married daughter—whose photograph on the wall would have graced the society page of any metropolitan daily. If mountain communities are the losers from such dispersal of their natives, I like to think that the nation at large gains—and that those who leave do not forget.

CERTAINLY all do not. About a hundred church or family reunions a year are held in the Smokies. The 54th gathering of the Sparks clan in 1979 drew 238 members.

In the 1830s Nathan and Jane Sparks became one of the first couples to settle in Cades Cove. Of the well-dressed assemblage of their descendants, I thought only Howard Sparks, born in the Cove in 1892 and now a lean six-foot-one, resembled the mountain man of popular lore. But he was not the oldest. The prize for that, a two-by-three-foot cake, went to Mrs. Carrie Franklin, a 91-year-old grande dame confined to a wheelchair by rheumatism—the penalty, perhaps, of homesteading in Colorado and Idaho. The youngest participant, only six weeks, won a cake for her parents; and a third cake went to Clifford Lawson of Mission, Texas, who had come the greatest distance.

The food the women had brought for the reunion picnic filled 90 feet of serving tables: ham, fried chicken, and barbecued steak; half a dozen vegetables; eight kinds of cake and five kinds of pie.

When I could neither eat any more nor move, I sat back and listened: "When Nathan saw those Confederates in the distance, he dropped the plow and took off on his best saddle horse, knowing they were likely to requisition it. He could hear a clatter behind him, and when he came to the end of the road he turned to face them. The noise was the workhorse with the plow bouncing behind it."

"One spring we were taking some horses to pasture on Spence Field when a mare slid halfway down to a creek," recounted Andy G. (Doc) Lane. "I tried to hold her where she was, but we went in together. And it was *cold*. There was a cabin on the mountain then, but when we got there my throat was closed with the croup, which used to kill a lot of children. My cousin boiled some lard, and while he sat on my chest my brother held my nose and poured it down me. I couldn't talk for three days, but after that I was all right."

"Uncle Tom Sparks was up on the ridge in the snow when he heard a screaming he thought was someone in trouble," Bob Wear said. "He followed the sound and a panther jumped on him. Maybe it had kits. He fought it off with a knife, slashing it behind a foreleg, but not before its claws had ripped him through five layers of clothes. Later little Willie Ore trapped it—knew it was Uncle Tom's by the scars. It was nine feet, nose to tail tip."

"Jane Sparks must have been near a hundred when she died. Her long life was generally attributed to what she called her toddy: whiskey with rock candy in the bottle." It was Bob Wear talking. "My brother was driving her in the hack one winter when the front wheel went off the edge of the road and pitched us into an icy creek. Grandma was up to her waist, but when I tried to help her she said never mind that, but get the bottle under the front seat. She refused to stop and change clothes when we got to a house, but thought she would have just a swallow of toddy. She was 95 then."

How shall I end? Perhaps, as I started, at Emerts Cove with Birgie Manning, who said in a voice so low only my wife, Vera, heard: "I just can't never forget them days."

*With strong hands and a sure touch, sculptor Goingback Chiltoskey fashions a wooden eagle at his home on the Cherokee reservation. Chiltoskey began carving at the age of 10. The North Carolina Cherokee descend from a group of about a thousand who in 1838 avoided the government's forcible removal to Oklahoma of more than 17,000 Indians from their ancestral homes in the southeastern United States.*

*Their property sold for the park in the late 1920s, Eva and Horace McCarter built this house just across the boundary. Such enduring ties to their mountain homeland persist among the people of the Great Smokies, people with deep roots in a pioneer past and fond memories of the days that "was much the best."*

# The Northern Appalachians

*Morning fog rising from a branch of Vermont's White River lingers over the peaceful valley.*

*By* Daniel E. Hutner
*Photographed by* Farrell Grehan *and* Sarah Leen

*Many New England mountainsides once cleared for farming have returned to forest.*

SARAH LEEN

MY FAVORITE STORY about the Green Mountains is one told by George Aiken, a Vermont politician and longtime friend of my grandfather. During the later years of the Great Depression, when Aiken was governor, some "boys from Washington" came up to the mountains and declared the farms submarginal. They offered to buy them and to provide loans so the farmers could relocate on better land. The Vermonters listened politely, talked among themselves, thanked the federal government's representatives for their interest—and declined.

In many ways, the spirit of the people who live in these mountains has changed little since the days of the Revolution when the British general John Burgoyne called them "the most active and most rebellious race of the continent." They embody the old Yankee virtues—thrift, self-reliance, industry, ingenuity, pride—with a touch of eccentricity and a large dose of what one native I know calls "contrariness." What shaped this spirit? Part of the answer, at least, is simple: the land.

The Green Mountains run in long ridges the length of Vermont. From the Champlain Valley they look more like hills than mountains, except for such distinct peaks as Mount Mansfield and Camels Hump. Some geologists speculate that this range, one of the oldest in the world, once stood as high as the Himalayas. But over a period of 300 to 400 million years, wind, water, and glacial ice have worn down the Green Mountains and given them a gentle, rounded look.

Never does the name of these mountains seem more fitting than in the spring. Day by day the fresh green climbs the hillsides, gradually turning a darker shade. But winter doesn't give up easily, threatening again and again to return and making it a time of the most fickle weather imaginable. Commented Mark Twain: "In the spring I have counted one hundred and thirty-six different kinds of weather inside of four-and-twenty hours."

The clash of seasons was in full play in early March as I headed north on State Route 100, a two-lane road nicknamed "the skiers' highway" because it passes near most of the ski areas in Vermont. The morning sunlight dazzled me as it bounced off birch trees coated with ice from the previous night's storm. Soon the ice began to melt, falling in long sheaths that shattered on the frozen ground. At the edges of the fields, the willows had turned bright yellow. The air felt damp and warm. A mist hung over the swollen White River, surging with chunks of ice as it filled the valley with its roar.

The first settlers in Vermont farmed the hillsides in preference to the marshy or clay-laden valleys. For a time they were nearly self-sufficient, clearing well-drained fields from the forested slopes, using the timber for houses, building

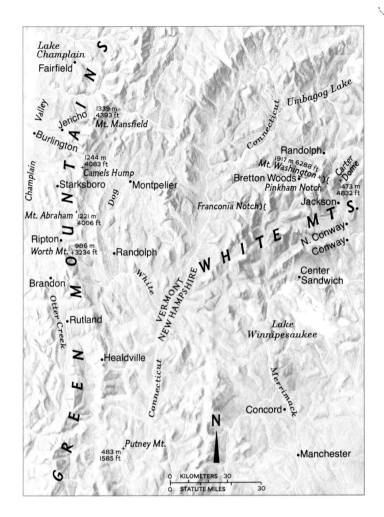

Map labels:
Lake Champlain
Fairfield
MOUNTAINS
Valley
Jericho
Burlington
1339 m 4393 ft
Mt. Mansfield
Champlain
1244 m 4083 ft
Camels Hump
Starksboro
Dog
Montpelier
Mt. Abraham +1221 m 4006 ft
Ripton
Worth Mt. 986 m +3234 ft
Randolph
White
VERMONT NEW HAMPSHIRE
Brandon
Otter Creek
Rutland
GREEN MOUNTAINS
Healdville
Connecticut
Putney Mt. 483 m 1585 ft
N
Connecticut Umbagog Lake
Randolph
Mt. Washington 1917 m 6288 ft
Bretton Woods
Pinkham Notch
Franconia Notch
Carter Dome 1473 m 4832 ft
Jackson
N. Conway
Conway
WHITE MTS.
Center Sandwich
Lake Winnipesaukee
Merrimack
Concord
Manchester

0 KILOMETERS 30
0 STATUTE MILES 30

*Two major ranges of the northern Appalachians, the Green Mountains and the White Mountains, have strongly influenced the history of Vermont and New Hampshire. Settled since colonial times, these New England highlands harbor quiet towns, small farms, and vacation cottages. National forests now protect large portions of both mountain ranges.*

walls with the rocks turned up by their plows, and raising much of their own food. But cultivation soon depleted the thin hill soil. When, in the early 1800s, a Vermonter serving as consul in Portugal sent home 4,000 Merino sheep—famous for their fine wool—many farmers decided their land was better used for pasture, and began improving their herds as a cash crop. By 1840 Vermont had become one of the world's leading wool-producing areas.

Within a few decades, however, many of the growers could no longer compete with lower-priced wool from the Midwest, and after the Civil War most of them switched to dairying. But again they found it increasingly difficult to meet the competition of larger, more efficient farms elsewhere.

"From the late 1860s on, mountain farming in Vermont declined steadily," said Tom Bahre, the Addison County forester. "New technology further reduced the number of small mountain farmers. Large machines just weren't practical on

ALL BY FARRELL GREHAN

182

Maple sugaring marks
the beginning of spring
on the Howrigan farm
near Fairfield, Vermont.
The right combination
of warm days and
freezing nights starts
the sap rising in maple
trees. Below, Lawrence
Howrigan drills a tap hole
for a spout. In another
part of the woods his
brother Kevin collects the
sap and pours it into a
gathering tank mounted

on a horse-drawn sleigh.
Opposite, above, steam
envelops the men as they
deliver sap for transfer
to storage tanks. Sales of
maple syrup provide
important income for
farmers at a season
of limited cash flow.

steep slopes. Besides, most couldn't make that kind of investment. The timberlands began to grow back up. At one point 75 percent of the land had been cleared; today 75 percent of the state is forest."

My old friend Larry Shepard knows the stern realities of mountain farming. I ran into him at the Addison County agricultural extension office, where he had come for information about a loan. I spent the rest of the day at his 280-acre place at Starksboro. The farm, unworked for nearly 20 years, had belonged to his grandfather. In 1976, Larry and his wife, Susan, decided to bring it back to life.

Their "diversified farming" approach is as old as the idea of a self-sufficient family farm. They have a few cows, chickens, pigs, goats, ducks—"enough of each to meet our own needs." They plant a vegetable garden and pick apples in the old orchard. To earn cash, they raise raspberries—500 quarts last year—and do some maple sugaring. And to keep costs down, Larry relies on his own skills for work like plumbing or carpentry, or makes some sort of trade with a friend. While we waited for dinner, Charley Barnes, an electrician, and his wife, Betty, dropped by. Charley had installed the wiring to Larry's barns. In exchange, Larry delivered a cord of firewood.

For extra income, "I'm building an addition on a house trailer down the road," Larry said. "Taking outside jobs is the only way we can get by for now. But it'll be worth all the sacrifice when we get this place in shape."

Standing by the garden, watching sunset color the mountains, I felt the enthusiasm that represented more than just an optimistic time of year. Susan came out of the house carrying their ten-month-old son, Nathan. As dusk settled softly, we reflected on one of those happy moments of farm life: Earlier that day, Epa, the alpine dairy goat, had given birth to a wobbly-legged kid.

My hopes for the Shepards' success were reinforced when I visited Harold Howrigan's 700-acre dairy farm near Fairfield. Harold is one of the largest maple syrup producers in the state. When the sap begins to flow, everyone pitches in—Harold's wife, two daughters, three sons. But now it was late in the season, and they were boiling off the last run.

The Howrigans' sugaring operation is an interesting blend of old and new. They rely on traditional methods, hanging buckets from spouts placed in the trees and using a gathering tank on a horse-drawn sleigh. But they also have an extensive system of plastic tubing for conveying the sap from holding tank to storage tank. I asked Harold why he continued to use the old methods. "I've been doing this all my life," he said. "And my father and his father did it before me. I just hate to give it up."

We walked behind the sugarhouse, where he showed me a wooden trough carved by his grandfather that funneled the sap into a 6,000-gallon stainless-steel storage tank.

Inside, while keeping an eye on the boiling sap, Harold explained the sugaring process. Sap flows from the storage tank into either of two boiling pans, which sit on furnaces called arches. In each pan, the sap passes through narrow channels, bubbling and frothing, becoming a rich amber color along the way. When it reaches the last section of the pan, Harold tests it with a hydrometer. "I try to be scientific about it," he said. "But it's mostly a matter of experience. You get so you just know when it's time to draw some off."

It often takes 40 to 50 gallons of sap to make a gallon of maple syrup. But one sip told me it was worth all the effort. "That's nature's finest," Harold said. The warm, sweet taste lingered on my lips long after I left the Howrigan farm.

IN 1865, A WEALTHY young man from Middlebury named Joseph Battell vacationed at a farm in Ripton. He enjoyed his stay so much that he bought the property. During the summers that followed, he invited friends to visit, and so many came that he decided to expand the place into an inn. But it was an unusual sort of inn, where guests often stayed the whole summer and had to ask for a bill. Battell had a special fondness for intellectuals, especially college professors like my great-grandfather Henry Cornwall. The Cornwalls were soon provided a cottage of their own.

One day Joseph Battell saw men cutting timber near the inn. Afraid of what this might portend for his beloved mountains, he began acquiring land. By the time he died in 1915, he owned about 36,000 acres—more than anyone else in Vermont—including every major peak from Worth Mountain to Camels Hump. Standing in front of the inn, he could boast that he owned every mountain in sight.

Today the Bread Loaf Inn and the surrounding mountains look much as they did at the turn of the century. The land is actually more heavily forested now that so many of the farms have disappeared. Battell bequeathed most of his holdings to Middlebury College. The school's trustees in turn sold more than 30,000 acres to the U. S. Forest Service for incorporation in the Green Mountain National Forest, but kept the inn and its surrounding land. Since the 1920s the inn has been the site of a graduate summer school of English and an annual writers' conference.

Walking by Cornwall Cottage during the 1979 conference, I remembered some of my grandfather's stories about Bread Loaf. How Joseph Battell, breeder of Morgan horses, long refused to allow cars on his land. How he built a small hotel near the summit of Mount (Continued on page 190)

FARRELL GREHAN

*Chunks of ice clutter the banks of the Dog River after Vermont's first thaw of the year. As the snow melts and river ice begins to break up, the streams swell with relentless force. Spring flooding often washes away roads and bridges and causes extensive damage to low-lying land.*

With ten-month-old Nathan on her back, Susan Shepard picks July wild flowers at Starksboro, Vermont. She and her husband, Larry, have spent the last 3½ years restoring the all-but-abandoned family farm. Below, Craig Ferguson carries strawberries he picked while working in the Robert Wood garden in Brandon, Vermont. On a hill farm near Randolph, Morgan Drury helps his father lead a purebred Morgan horse to a paddock. Schoolmaster Justin Morgan established the breed at Randolph in the 1820s. Throughout the mountains, newborn animals like the foal at far right signal the arrival of spring.

LEFT, ABOVE, AND BELOW: SARAH LEEN

186

At day's end Dick Collitt and his son, Matthew, retire the American flag displayed in front of the Ripton Country Store. The Collitts bought the store several years ago when they moved to the small mountain town of Ripton, Vermont. Working 12 hours a day, seven days a week, they sell a range of merchandise typical of the old-fashioned general store. The appeal of tradition also brought 79-year-old Randolph Smith to Vermont after a career in education. As head of the Crowley Cheese Factory at Healdville, he oversees a process for making Colby cheese that goes back more than a hundred years.

189

Abraham. How he named the peaks he owned after honorees ranging from President Lincoln's mother to himself.

I was glad to find that the sense of a distinctive summer community at Bread Loaf has survived. Although automobiles pass by on State Route 125, the inn remains somehow insulated from the outside world. Perhaps it is the location, a broad valley between two ridges of mountains. Perhaps it is the protective ghost of Joseph Battell.

The late Wilson A. Bentley had his own reasons for spending his life within the shelter of the Green Mountains. One was the region's frequent snowfalls.

I learned more about "Snowflake" Bentley one afternoon when I stopped at the Chittenden Mills, a historic site in Jericho. Bentley devoted himself to photographing the ice crystals that form snowflakes. Combining microscope and camera, he was the first person to develop a successful technique for taking photomicrographs of the delicate, transitory flakes. His hobby evolved into a lifetime preoccupation, and he became a world-renowned expert in his specialty. For many years artists and craftsmen, especially jewelers, have turned to his published collection for designs.

Like Snowflake Bentley and Joseph Battell, George Aiken has earned the respect of Vermonters for his independence and individuality. As governor, then as United States senator for 34 years, he became widely known for his understated humor, blunt honesty, and common sense.

I visited the 86-year-old retired statesman and his wife, Lola, at their farm near the top of Putney Mountain. We spent much of the time discussing two of his favorite subjects—politics and gardening—and I asked how he lasted all those years in Washington. "It was sort of like being in exile," he acknowledged. "Of course, I had a lot of fun, too. Meeting the leaders of other countries and all that. But I'm a hill farmer at heart. It's good to be back."

FOR A RANGE so close to the Green Mountains, the White Mountains could hardly be more dissimilar. Many of the human activities there are the same—maple sugaring, lumbering, farming, outdoor recreation. But driving north on New Hampshire Route 16 in April, I was struck by the abrupt change in the landscape.

"The scenery in Conway and onward to North Conway is surprisingly grand," wrote Henry Thoreau in his journal. "Often from the midst of level maple groves . . . you look out . . . to the most rugged scenery in New England."

Younger than the Green Mountains, the White Mountains formed as clusters of peaks in what is now north central New Hampshire, spilling over into Maine, Vermont, and Quebec. More than 30 of the New Hampshire peaks are taller than the highest of the Green Mountains, though by less than 2,000 feet. In general they are composed of metamorphosed sedimentary rock that has been folded, then penetrated by magma intrusions, leaving an abundance of visible granite that has given New Hampshire its nickname of the Granite State.

Mount Washington, the range's dominant peak (6,288 feet), undergoes some of the worst weather in the world outside the polar regions. The cause is a combination of height and location where several major storm tracks meet. The weather observatory at the summit records hurricane-force gusts nearly every month of the year. Because of the harsh conditions, timberline is low—about 5,200 feet.

Snow and ice on these mountains often last well into June. Even when the snow has melted, the bald, mica-studded summit of Mount Washington appears nearly white: the reason, presumably, not only for its early name of Crystal Hill but also for the term White Mountains. Despite their relatively low elevation—Robert Frost observed that New Hampshire's mountains "aren't quite high enough"—to me they have the *feel* of the greatest peaks.

That certainly was true late one afternoon as I stood on the headwall of Tuckerman Ravine, a vast bowl carved by glaciers below the summit of Mount Washington. My legs began to tremble from fear as I put on my skis. I tried not to look down at the white slope below, which in places reaches a pitch of 55°—one of the steepest ski runs in the world.

The air turned cold as a cloud bank swept over the ridge. Soon the snow, temporarily softened by the sun, would be hard as ice. Water trickled from a rock nearby into the depths of a crevasse, where it made a low, gurgling sound.

I pushed off, stiff and breathless as I made quick turns down a narrow chute, then growing more relaxed and easing into smooth, wide turns, giving myself over to that sensation of speed that lies somewhere between flying and falling.

Skiing Tuckerman Ravine is a New England tradition, a rite of spring. Because the ravine has no lifts, skiers must hike a steep 3 1/4 miles from Pinkham Notch to reach the top of the headwall. More than 50 feet of snow normally accumulates in the ravine, assuring good skiing at least through May.

Wes Blake, at 77 still an active skier, told me the classic Tuckerman story about the April day in 1939 when Austrian champion Toni Matt, misjudging his location, schussed the headwall—skied straight down it without making any turns to control his speed, a feat assumed to be impossible.

"It was during the race called The Inferno. Toni skied directly down from the summit and plunged over the rim of the ravine onto the headwall. The spectators just stared. The whole ravine was still. He must have been going 100 miles an

*Lunchtime for foliage feeders: A young grasshopper rests on a fern; an eastern tent caterpillar inspects the broad leaf of a shrub. Insects become active later in the mountains than in the valleys below; spring takes about a month to work its way up the slopes of the Green Mountains.*

hour. Once safely at the bottom, at Pinkham Notch, he'd broken the old course record by half."

Skiing is just one of many forms of recreation pursued in the White Mountains. Hiking, canoeing, kayaking, swimming, fishing, hunting, ice and rock climbing, ski touring, snowmobiling—all draw thousands of visitors each year. But the greatest attraction by far is the scenery.

Niels Nielsen took me to New Hampshire's most famous tourist stop, a rock profile in Franconia Notch called the Old Man of the Mountain. Niels, an affable, bear-size man, works as the head of a repair crew for the New Hampshire Department of Public Works and Highways. Expertise gained overseeing maintenance of all state bridges north of Franconia Notch has helped Niels with his other major responsibility: making sure the Old Man doesn't fall.

In the 1870s, Appalachian Mountain Club members discovered that the forehead boulder seemed about to slip. But not until 1916 were rods and turnbuckles installed to hold the boulder in place. "A lot of work has been done since then," said Niels, as we gazed up at the Old Man. The profile is seen best along a hundred-yard stretch of U. S. Route 3. "Every year we test the turnbuckles, and check for any movement. I also sealed some cracks with wire mesh coated with epoxy to keep water from getting in and freezing."

I sensed that much more than tourist dollars is involved in the effort to preserve the Old Man. "I'm very moved every time I see him," said Niels. "I find it hard to believe such a likeness could just happen." I asked how long he expected the rocks to hold. "Who knows? I'll feel I've succeeded if he lasts for another generation," Niels said.

TOURISM has been a major industry in the White Mountains ever since the region's railroads were built and the Grand Hotel Era began about 1870. People from the cities of the East traveled northward to escape the summer heat. Often they lived a life of luxury, with servants, black-tie dinners, the finest entertainment. As I drove through the mountains, I saw the shells of old hotel buildings, some with as many as 300 rooms. But the Mount Washington Hotel at Bretton Woods still operates. Its size and Spanish Renaissance architecture make it a striking sight at the foot of the Presidential Range. It is probably best known for the international monetary conference held here in 1944.

With Tom Deans, executive director of the Appalachian Mountain Club, I stood on the porch of the hotel and looked out over a recent addition to the White Mountain National Forest—the 6,600-acre Bretton Woods parcel. "Developers wanted to build a recreation community for 25,000 people out there," explained Tom. "Hikers in the mountains would

have been looking down on houses instead of trees. Obviously, the AMC opposed that sort of development. We worked hard to help the Forest Service acquire this land."

Volunteer organizations like the Appalachian Mountain Club and the Society for the Protection of New Hampshire Forests played a major role in the creation and expansion of the White Mountain National Forest. Its establishment was made possible by the Weeks Act of 1911; more than half of its present area had been purchased by 1924.

"People around here feel a real sense of pride and responsibility when it comes to the forest," Tom said. "We have seen the damage that can happen when special interests like lumbering control the land. And we don't want it to happen again. I'd say the people around here have learned how to cooperate to protect their mountains."

Tom, who grew up on the Maine coast, first came to the White Mountains with his grandfather to hike. "A lot of AMC families go back several generations. We're the oldest organization of our kind in the country. I think that's what makes these mountains different from some of the ranges out west; people were coming here for recreation when they were still being explored. It's what I call a 'heritage of use,' an attachment I hope to pass on to my children."

Later I spent a night at Greenleaf Hut, part of the AMC system of eight huts in the White Mountains located a day's hike apart. The huts offer meals, bunks, and companionship—a welcome luxury for the weary hiker. Crews of college-age men and women operate the *(Continued on page 198)*

*Highest peak east of the Mississippi and north of the Carolinas, 6,288-foot Mount Washington looks deceptively peaceful in the spring dawn. Often shrouded in clouds, the New Hampshire monarch has become notorious for its bitter weather. Temperatures can drop below freezing and winds reach hurricane force any month of the year. Rangers warn hikers to turn back at the first sign of a storm.*

FOLLOWING PAGES:
*Lost Pond, near Pinkham Notch, reflects the racing clouds of a bright May day. Mountains in the distance still hold a few patches of snow.*

FARRELL GREHAN

*Austere terrain surrounds
Lakes of the Clouds
Hut. Located above tree
line and just below the
summit of Mount Monroe,
the hut gets its name from
two alpine tarns. Inside,
Dawson Winch ladles beef
soup for hungry hikers.
College-age crews operate
eight such huts in summer
for the Appalachian
Mountain Club. Nearby,
on the upper slopes of
Mount Washington,
botanist Gerard Courtin
studies the tundra
vegetation. Tiny bells of
moss plant and drifts
of alpine bluet bloom there
almost as soon as
the snow melts.*

197

huts, packing much of the food and supplies up steep trails.

Tom Deans began his 25-year career with the Appalachian Mountain Club at Greenleaf Hut. Posted on the wall are the following records from Franconia Notch:

*179 lbs., 2 hours: 28 minutes, 1960  Tom Deans*
Quick Trips:
*55 lbs., 49 minutes, 1959  Tom Deans*

I will add that although I am in good physical condition, it took me, with only a light pack, 3 1/2 hours to reach the hut.

IN SOME SITUATIONS, of course, speed on the trail is quite beside the point. The day I spent climbing Carter Dome with Scott MacLachlan, a graduate student in wildlife ecology at the University of New Hampshire, my companion spent much of his time photographing spring ephemerals—briefly flowering plants many of which are rare and protected species. Normally I like to hike fast, but Scott made me slow down—and look—and *see*.

Forest and mountains came into focus for me in a way they never had before. I noticed how the trail had been damaged by heavy use. I touched marks left on a tree trunk by ice in a swollen stream. I spied sprays of club moss peeking through the woodland carpet, and tasted leaves of Labrador tea.

When we finally reached the summit, we could see full circle: the white snow on other peaks, the green of the valleys, the endless blue ridges disappearing in the haze. To the east lay the Wild River watershed, a large roadless area of the White Mountain National Forest.

"Wilderness areas are the big controversy up here right now," Bruce Cairns, a hunting guide, told us later at his home in Randolph. "Some people want to set aside large tracts of forest land to be tightly controlled under the Wilderness Act. No other issue has so divided folks here."

Scott had met Bruce at a hearing on bobcats, animals so elusive that wildlife biologists rarely get a chance to see one. Scott, who is writing his master's thesis on the habits of bobcats, found he could learn a lot from woodsmen like Bruce.

"I'm all for wilderness," said Bruce. "But in some cases I think that classification is unnecessary. There are other ways already in effect to protect the forest: enlightened lumbering practices, strictly enforced regulations on recreational use. It's a question of continuing proper management.

"These mountains are wilder today than they have been in years," he added. "A friend of mine tells me he spotted a mountain lion recently."

To me the most unspoiled, natural area of all in the White Mountains is several square miles of alpine tundra at the top of Mount Washington. Not that I didn't see plenty of signs of civilization nearby. Men were hard at work on a new summit building that will augment the present structures—weather observatory, television and radio stations, power generator, and a former hotel called the Tip Top House. An eight-mile road winds up one side of the mountain, while a cog railway climbs the other. Every year more than a quarter of a million people reach the top. Yet close at hand is a special place few of these visitors ever see. Dr. Gerard Courtin, professor of botany at Laurentian University in Ontario, took me there early in June. An expert in alpine ecology, Gerry is very familiar with the Alpine Garden, an area containing a fragile community of tundra plants.

As we walked down the road, Gerry suddenly took off, leaping from rock to rock in his orange parka and black beret, his daypack flapping in the 40-mile-an-hour wind. "Come here," he commanded, crouching over a strip of dark green. "Moss campion. See the tiny purple flowers?"

Then he was off again, leading me down the other side of the ridge. We stopped beside something that looked like a low, shrubby hedge. "A balsam fir," said Gerry. "At about 4,500 feet, these trees are prevented from growing upright by wind and by blowing snow that is too abrasive for the young shoots; so they begin to grow sideways. This little tree is probably more than a hundred years old."

Above us rose the cone of Mount Washington, a heap of light-gray stone. But here, soil saturated during the spring thaw had concentrated among the rocks to form small terraces where plants could grow. I bent low to inspect them. Three-forked rush tossed in the wind. Mountain cranberry had a tart taste; goldthread had sepals as smooth as butter.

A white-flowering plant called sandwort grew on the trail. "It's a pioneer plant," said Gerry, "one of the first to return to damaged areas. On a moonlit night it's easy to pick out the trail by the reflection from the masses of petals."

Heading back, we reached a spot not more than 50 feet from the summit where the trail leveled out. "The snow left here only ten days ago," Gerry said. "In winter it blows off the summit and piles up here." At our feet we saw the most beautiful flower of all—the blossom of the dwarf shrub called moss plant. "Snow protects these plants. This whole scene is continually resculptured by the presence or absence of snow." He smiled. "Each plant finds its own niche."

And, I thought, the people who live in these New England mountains have found their own niche, too. As times change, they keep finding a way to get by. And all so they can stay up among their hills and hollows, peaks and valleys. Why? Perhaps George Aiken had the best answer in his book *Speaking From Vermont:*

"It isn't just scenery that attracts people to New England. It is a realization of fundamental values of life."

*Striped or "goosefoot" maple, a large shrub or small tree, takes its nickname from the shape of its leaves. Interrupted fern (opposite) appears early in the spring in rocky fields and along stone walls. Both plants occur as natives throughout New England.*

*Golf course in summer, cross-country ski area in winter: These open lands in Jackson, New Hampshire, lie at the heart of one of the largest complexes of maintained ski trails in the United States. Otto Ninow (opposite) heads the ski patrol at one of the five downhill ski areas around Jackson. Owner of a*

*music store, he can play*
*every instrument he sells.*
*At right, firewood stacked*
*beside a Conway home*
*awaits the cold winter.*

*Church towers rise above well-kept white clapboard houses in the village of Center Sandwich, New Hampshire. Insulated from resort development by its distance from main travel routes, the town attempts to preserve the atmosphere of New England's past. A planning board enforces strict building and zoning regulations. At left, Ben Lear stops to chat with David McLaughry as he mends a fence beneath purple lilacs in full bloom.*

## Notes on Contributors

JAMES P. BLAIR has been a National Geographic Society photographer since 1962. In 1978 he received the award of the Overseas Press Club for Best Photographic Reporting From Abroad for his coverage of South Africa. He is presently working on a major coverage of the disappearing tropical forest.

A former writer and editor for NATIONAL GEOGRAPHIC, free-lance journalist LOUIS DE LA HABA is a frequent contributor to Special Publications. He is a graduate of Amherst College and earned an M.A. degree in anthropology from George Washington University.

NICHOLAS DEVORE III lives in Aspen, Colorado, where he formerly served as a forest ranger in the Maroon Bells-Snowmass Wilderness. His photographs have appeared in NATIONAL GEOGRAPHIC and numerous other publications.

Born in Vancouver, British Columbia, DAVID FALCONER moved to Portland, Oregon, as a small boy. For 25 years—until 1979—he was a photographer for the *Oregonian;* he also has taught photojournalism at Portland State University.

RALPH GRAY is the editor of WORLD, National Geographic's monthly magazine for children. A staff member since 1943 and author of many GEOGRAPHIC articles, he served as Chief of the School Service and editor of the *School Bulletin* until WORLD began publication in 1975.

A trip to Grand Teton National Park in 1967 resulted in a new hobby—mountaineering—for National Geographic writer-researcher SALLIE M. GREENWOOD. Her avocation has drawn her to peaks from the Peruvian Andes to the Pamirs of Soviet Central Asia.

New Yorker FARRELL GREHAN, trained as a painter and sculptor, turned to photography in 1954. His work for NATIONAL GEOGRAPHIC has included articles on roses, tulips, and wilderness areas. He photographed the 1976 Special Publication *John Muir's Wild America.*

ANNIE GRIFFITHS, a native of Minneapolis, graduated from the University of Minnesota with a degree in photojournalism. Her present assignments include photographing several chapters for upcoming Books for World Explorers, published by National Geographic.

Free-lance writer DANIEL E. HUTNER grew up in Princeton, New Jersey, and lived in Vermont after graduating in 1970 from Middlebury College. He later received an M.A. in English from the University of Virginia. He has contributed to a number of the Society's publications.

SARAH LEEN, born in Wisconsin, is a staff photographer for the Topeka *Capital Journal* in Kansas. While attending the University of Missouri Graduate School of Journalism, she was honored as the 1979 College Photographer of the Year.

National Geographic writer-photographer GEORGE F. MOBLEY has traveled the world since joining the Society's staff in 1961. Between assignments, he lives on a small farm in the shadow of northwestern Virginia's Massanutten Mountain.

"I enjoy mountain wilderness," says H. ROBERT MORRISON, "for its breathtaking scenery and the challenge of a demanding environment." A graduate of Howard University in Washington, D. C., he has been a member of the Society's staff since 1964.

Widely known as a nature writer, CHARLTON OGBURN has contributed to the Special Publications *As We Live and Breathe: The Challenge of Our Environment* and *American Mountain People.* He is the author of more than a dozen books, including National Geographic's *Railroads: The Great American Adventure.*

"Although I grew up in New York City, I have always felt at home in the mountains," says CYNTHIA RUSS RAMSAY. A graduate of Hunter College and a contributor to many Special Publications, she has also been managing editor of the Society's Books for Young Explorers.

Mountaineer GALEN ROWELL, who made the first skiing circumnavigation of Mount McKinley and the first one-day climb to its summit, is credited with more than a hundred first ascents. He has written and photographed two books published by the Sierra Club.

## Acknowledgments

The Special Publications Division is grateful to the individuals and organizations named or quoted in the text and to those listed here for their generous cooperation and assistance during the preparation of this book: American Alpine Club, the Geological Survey of Canada, Eddie Leivas, the Embassy of Mexico, the National Park Service, Carroll L. Riley, Robert H. Schmidt, the Smithsonian Institution, Smoky Mountain Historical Society, and the U. S. Forest Service.

FARRELL GREHAN

*Mount Rainier, Washington, towers above lesser peaks of the Cascade Range. After his ascent in 1888, naturalist John Muir called Rainier "so fine and so beautiful it might well fire the dullest observer to desperate enthusiasm."*

Composition for *America's Magnificent Mountains* by National Geographic's Photographic Services, Carl M. Shrader, Chief, Lawrence F. Ludwig, Assistant Chief. Printed and bound by Holladay-Tyler Printing Corp., Rockville, Md. Color separations by The Lanman Companies, Washington, D. C.; National Bickford Graphics, Inc., Providence, R.I.; Progressive Color Corp., Rockville, Md.; and The J. Wm. Reed Co., Alexandria, Va.

# Index

Boldface indicates illustrations;
*italic* refers to picture legends
(captions)

**Library of Congress CIP Data**

National Geographic Society,
Washington, D. C. Special
Publications Division.
America's magnificent mountains.

Includes index.
1. Mountains—United States. 2.
Coast Mountains—Description and
travel. 3. Sierra Madre Mountains,
Mexico—Description and travel. 4.
United States—Description and
travel—1960-    I. Title.
E169.02.N37 1980    917.3    78-21447
ISBN 0-87044-281-3, regular binding
ISBN 0-87044-286-4, library binding